Spices, Rices
and other Vices

a cookbook

from Miami and the Beach

BEVERLY JOHNSON PENZELL • MARCIA RABINOWITZ • JACQUELINE SIMKIN

BARRICADE
BOOKS

ACKNOWLEDGMENTS

We wish to express appreciation to Jesus Acosta, Livvy Aftanas, Maggie Aguiar, Geila Rosen Blank, Maria Elena Cardenas, Juan Chardiet, Eleanor Chochinov, Marisela Cisneros, Diane Simkin Demeter, Norma Espinosa, Maria Fenton, Ofra Granatman, Robert Gross, Faye Haberman, Peter Haberman, Aunt Delia Haldane, Katherine Rita Johnson, Joy Kaufman, Judy Keefe, Maureen Marsch, Anita Ruth Schwartz Neville, Ann Ostrow, Donna Penzell, Marina Polvay, Ginger Schwartz Posnick, Selma Rabinowitz, Gretta Ritter, Susan Santoro, Gerhard Schmeid, Alex Silvestre, Blackie Simkin, Claribel Simkin, Ann Tannenbaum, Joan Teper, Ruthie Teper, Shirley Zoloth, our families, friends and others offering culinary inspiration, professional advice and/or encouragement to see this cookbook in print.

Preface

Miami is a sizzling, sensational city, a marvelous, multicultural mecca whose community is hot-tempered, exciting, explosive and romantic. The influences here on both culture and cuisine are very diverse; however, the major currents are American and Latin American, as reflected in the pages of this cookbook. A strong impetus for the book was not only to document our favorite creations and traditions, but also to advance an integration of Miami's cultures through food.

This cookbook is an eclectic collection of our creations, traditional foods, and time-tried favorite recipes shared with us by our mothers, sisters, brothers, aunts, uncles, cousins and friends.

Although many of us have, at some time, thought how much fun it would be to experiment with food, entertain with ease and cook for our families daily without feeling its drudgery, the task seems to become more and more complex in the nineties. Most of us are finding that the demands of both work and family can be enormous, with leisure time minimal. At the same time we are rediscovering the joys of relaxing and entertaining at home.

Our book is designed to help you successfully juggle these competing interests in a creative way. We include practical, easy-to-follow recipes which are simple to prepare and elegant to serve; which will have family appeal and provide pleasure for your friends. Most of the recipes consist of fresh ingredients easily found in your local market or ingredients you would normally keep in your home. The intent is to provide recipes which require little advance planning, as well as a few others which are more intricate, for special occasions, or for those times when you look forward to a challenge in the kitchen.

Beverly, a native of Miami, brought the three of us together knowing we each share a passionate love for cooking creatively, nurturing family and friends, and entertaining graciously. As the sometimes unique combination of ingredients are blended to create great recipes of the New American Cuisine, we have combined our talents to present this cookbook. In addition to each of us equally contributing to the recipes, we each have contributed to the creation of the book. Beverly coordinated production and editing, Marcia developed the illustrations, layout and artistic design, and Jackie contributed the photography in collaboration with photographer Barry Howe.

We hope you have as much pleasure in preparing and sharing these recipes as we have had in bringing them to you.

Enjoy!

Beverly Johnson Penzell
Marcia Kanengiser Rabinowitz
Jacqueline Simkin

Book Design and Illustrations – Marcia Rabinowitz
Front Cover – Marcia Rabinowitz
Photographs: pages 6, 8, 17, 21, 25, 34, 39, 51, 55, 59, 67, 71, 87, 99, 103, 121, 137, 141, 157, 177, 185, 189, 197, 206 – Jacqueline Simkin
Photographs: pages 3, 4, 43, 117, 132, 133, 162, 163, 171, 175 – Barry Howe
Recipes edited by Marina Polvay

Published by Barricade Books Inc.
1530 Palisade Avenue
Fort Lee, NJ 07024

Distributed by Publishers Group West
4065 Hollis
Emeryville, CA 94608

Manufactured in Hong Kong by Blaze IPI.

Library of Congress Cataloging-in-Publication Data

Penzell, Beverly Johnson.
  Spices, rices and other vices: a cookbook from Miami and the beach / by Beverly Johnson Penzell, Marcia Rabinowitz, Jacqueline Simkin.
  Includes index.
  ISBN 0-942637-91-7
  1. Cookery, American 2. Cookery—Florida—Miami. I. Rabinowitz, Marcia II. Simkin, Jacqueline III. Title
TX715.P4644 1993   92-46083
641.5973—dc20   CIP

0 9 8 7 6 5 4 3 2 1

DEDICATION

In loving memory of my mother, Katherine Rita Johnson, and to my husband Kris and daughter, Jessica Joy – Beverly

For my grandmothers Rusie Katz and Fanny Simkin, my sister Diane Demeter, my nieces Sara and Nikki, and especially for my wonderful mother, Claribel Simkin – Jacqueline

To my beautiful family: my husband Mark, son David Ian and daughter Jordana Michael – Marcia

Table of contents

Hors D' Oeuvres

ASPARAGUS SOUFFLÉ

3 tablespoons butter
4 tablespoons all-purpose flour
1½ cups milk
6 egg yolks
1 tablespoon fresh parsley, chopped
1 tablespoon fresh chives, chopped
salt and pepper to taste
4 to 5 tablespoons Parmesan cheese, grated
1 cup asparagus tops, cooked al dente and cut into pieces
pinch cream of tartar
8 egg whites, room temperature

1. Preheat oven to 350°F. Butter a six cup soufflé dish and tie a collar* around it.

2. Melt butter and add flour, stirring until smooth. Slowly whisk in milk until sauce is smooth and thick. Remove from heat.

3. Whisk in egg yolks, one at a time.

4. Add parsley, chives, salt, pepper, cheese and asparagus pieces.

5. Add a pinch of cream of tartar to egg whites and beat until stiff but not dry.

6. Mix a few heaping spoonfuls of the egg whites into the sauce to make it lighter and then fold in the rest with care.

7. Place mixture in soufflé dish and cook 35 to 40 minutes.

Serves 4.

*To make a collar, cut a strip of wax paper five inches wide and long enough to surround the soufflé dish. Butter the inside of collar and stick around top edge of the dish.

HOT DILL SAUCE

3 tablespoons butter
3 tablespoons flour
1 cup vegetable broth, hot
1 cup milk
4 tablespoons fresh dill, chopped, or 2 tablespoons dried
2 to 3 tablespoons dry Sherry
salt and pepper to taste

1. Make a roux by melting butter in saucepan, add flour and mix until smooth. Whisk in hot broth.

2. Stirring, add milk and let it cook over very low heat a few minutes.

3. Add dill and Sherry, season with salt and pepper and cook, stirring, 10 minutes. Serve hot over asparagus *soufflé*.

Makes 2 cups.

SESAME EGGPLANT DIP

Delicious with bread sticks or crackers. Or try topping toasted bread points with this dip sprinkled with Parmesan cheese as an accompaniment to soups.

1 large eggplant
3 tablespoons sesame seeds
¼ cup sour cream
1 clove garlic, crushed
1 teaspoon lemon juice
⅛ teaspoon creole seasoning (see page 87)

1. Preheat oven to 350°F.
2. Pierce eggplant with fork and bake one hour, or until very soft. Let cool.
3. Increase oven temperature to 375°F.
4. Spread sesame seeds one layer deep in small, shallow pan and toast 8 to 10 minutes, or until browned, turning frequently. Set aside.
5. Scoop pulp from eggplant and mash well. Add sour cream, garlic, lemon juice, seasoning and half the sesame seeds. Mix well.
6. Transfer to serving dish and top with remaining sesame seeds.

Makes 1½ cups.

GUACAMOLE

Guacamole is a chunky salad best made with a knife rather than food processor.

½ small, red onion
2 tomatoes
4 large avocados, peeled, pit removed
3 garlic cloves, minced
2 tablespoons olive oil
6 tablespoons lime juice
salt and pepper to taste
2 fresh jalepeño peppers, seeded and chopped (optional)
3 teaspoons mayonnaise (optional)

1. Cut onion, tomato and avocado into rough ½-inch chunks, mash in bowl with fork and add remaining seasonings.
2. For spicier guacamole, add jalepeño peppers.
3. For creamier guacamole, add mayonnaise.

Makes 4 cups.

CRAB-STUFFED WHOLE ARTICHOKES

2 large fresh artichokes, trimmed
1 fresh lemon, cut in half
½ cup crab salad (market prepared or Lily's Lobster Salad, page 57)
½ cup Parmesan cheese, grated

1. Trim artichokes by slicing off stem and pulling off outer lower leaves. With scissors, snip tips off remaining leaves and with a knife, cut off top one-third of artichoke.

2. Coat tips and bottom with lemon juice to avoid browning.

3. Bring large pot of water to a boil, add artichokes and leftover lemon; boil gently 25 to 45 minutes, until bottom is tender when pierced with a fork and a center petal pulls off easily. Drain upside down and let cool enough to handle.

4. Spread leaves open and remove fibrous choke in center. (A grapefruit spoon works well to separate the choke from the heart – the best part). Place ¼ cup crab salad inside each cavity and sprinkle with some Parmesan cheese. Separate outer leaves and sprinkle with remaining Parmesan cheese. Close leaves back to center.

5. Preheat oven to 400°F.

6. Bake 10 minutes or until thoroughly warmed and cheese is melted. Serve in separate small bowls placed on larger plates to hold petals after eating artichoke pulp.

7. To eat, start from the bottom and pull off petals one by one. Pull through teeth to scrape off soft, pulpy portion and melted cheese from the petals. The remaining heart topped with crab is completely edible and worth waiting for.

Serves 2.

Variations: *Prepare as directed through #3 above; discard all outer petals and choke. Top each artichoke heart with 1 tablespoon goat cheese mixed with a sprinkling of thyme and fresh garlic. Bake 15 minutes in a 375°F. preheated oven. A simple method is to trim, cook and drain artichokes; spread petals, sprinkle with Parmesan cheese and serve. The choke can be removed at the table.*

ORIENTAL SCALLION DIP

Serve with sturdy vegetables such as carrots, celery sticks, cauliflower or broccoli florets. Also good as a salad dressing.

½ cup tofu
½ cup scallions, finely chopped
¼ cup fresh parsley, chopped
2 tablespoons walnuts, chopped
1 tablespoon Tamari sauce
½ teaspoon cumin
1 cup plain yogurt

    1. Blend all ingredients, except yogurt, in blender or food processor until well mixed.
    2. Fold in yogurt and chill before serving.

Makes 1¾ cups.

CREOLE ARTICHOKE DIP

1 14-ounce can artichokes, drained
1 small onion
¾ cup mayonnaise
1 cup Parmesan cheese, freshly grated
1 clove garlic, crushed
¼ teaspoon Creole Seasoning (see page 87)
fresh parsley, minced, for garnish
paprika for garnish

    1. Preheat oven to 350°F.
    2. Purée all ingredients in food processor or blender.
    3. Transfer to ovenproof serving dish and bake 20 minutes. Serve warm with chips, crackers or vegetables.

Makes 2½ cups.

BROILED FLORIDA GRAPEFRUIT

6 chicken livers
3 grapefruits, halved
1 cup brown sugar, or more as needed

1. Broil chicken livers until still pink inside.
2. Cut in half and section grapefruits.
3. Sprinkle enough brown sugar over top to coat well.
4. Broil until edges are slightly brown.
5. Place broiled chicken liver in center of grapefruit.

Serves 6.

VEGETABLE PATÉ

Even those who usually avoid paté reach for more of this.

½ cup onions, minced
1 tablespoon butter
2 cups green beans, steamed
½ cup walnuts, toasted
2 hard-boiled eggs
2 tablespoons plain yogurt
2 tablespoons Brandy
¼ teaspoon salt
¼ teaspoon freshly ground pepper
⅛ teaspoon nutmeg

1. Sauté onions in butter and set aside.
2. Combine all ingredients in food processor or blender until smooth.
3. Transfer to a mold and chill. Unmold and serve as a spread for crackers or thinly sliced french bread.

Makes 2½ cups.

SPINACH BOUREKAS

Phyllo dough, defrosted
1 pound fresh spinach or ½ pound frozen chopped spinach
1 onion, chopped
1 tablespoon olive oil or butter for browning
2½ tablespoons pine nuts, browned
¼ pound Gruyere or Emmenthaler cheese, grated
1 egg, lightly beaten
2 tablespoons raisins
freshly ground black pepper to taste
pinch nutmeg
½ cup butter, melted (see page 155)
3 tablespoons sesame seeds

1. Preheat oven to 250°F. Trim stems from fresh spinach. Wash, drain and chop. If frozen spinach is used, defrost and drain water.

2. Sauté onion in oil or butter until soft. Add spinach and simmer in its own juice until tender.

3. Brown pine nuts in oven 7 to 10 minutes, turning frequently.

4. Stir pine nuts, grated cheese, beaten egg, raisins, pepper and nutmeg into spinach mixture.

5. Preheat oven to 425°F.

6. To fill Phyllo dough, spread damp towel on kitchen counter or cutting board, place one leaf on towel and brush with melted butter using pastry brush. Place second leaf over first and brush again with butter. Continue this method until nine leaves have been used. Put filling on edge of dough nearest you in one strip and roll like a jelly roll. Transfer roll to greased cookie sheet, brush top with melted butter and sprinkle. kle with sesame seeds. Bake approximately 20 minutes or until dough is nicely browned. Slice into one inch pieces and serve.

Makes 16.

ANITA RUTH'S CAVIAR PATÉ

Since Jackie and Anita were four years old, they played and talked at Anita's beach cottage. Now they cook and talk there.

½ cup unsalted butter
2 cans (7 ounces each) water-packed tuna, drained
1 tablespoon chives, chopped
1 jar (8 ounces) herring tidbits in wine, drained
¼ teaspoon garlic powder
½ teaspoon sugar
1 tablespoon water
1 can (4 ounces) black caviar
1 can (4 ounces) red caviar
4 sprigs parsley
lemon slices

1. Melt butter and pour into blender.
2. Add tuna and blend.
3. Add chives, herring tidbits, garlic powder, sugar and water. Blend until smooth.
4. Put wax paper inside lightly greased round pan or bowl and pour in blended mixture. Refrigerate 2 hours.
5. To unmold, turn pan over onto a serving platter and take off wax paper.
6. Top the mold with black caviar and coat sides with red caviar. Garnish with parsley and lemon slices.

Serves 10.

GRETA'S CHEESE FONDUE

1 clove garlic
4 ounces dry white wine
3 ounces Appenzeller, Tilsit or Emmenthaler cheese, grated
6 ounces Gruyere cheese, grated
½ teaspoon potato flour
1 ounce Kirsh
freshly ground pepper to taste
pinch nutmeg
french bread

1. Cut garlic in half and rub inside fondue pot. Add wine and heat just to boiling but don't boil.

2. Add cheeses and keep simmering until dissolved. Add flour and keep stirring in the same direction with wooden spoon. Add Kirsh, pepper and nutmeg to taste.

3. Stir another 5 minutes. The mixture should be bubbling.

4. To serve, break french bread, cuban bread, or carambola (star fruit) or tangelo into pieces and dip into fondue with fondue forks.

Serves 4.

AREPAS VENEZUELAN STYLE

Bev and her husband became fascinated with these while visiting Venezuela. They were sold on nearly every street corner, filled with you name it...

*2 cups Arepas corn flour (Harina Masa – Precooked yellow cornmeal)
1 teaspoon salt
2 cups water, approximately
Pam, olive oil or butter

Garnishes to be served in individual bowls:

1 recipe black beans (see page 66)
Queso blanco, sliced (queso blanco means "white cheese"
    similar to Mozzarella, Muenster or Farmer's cheese)
2 ripe tomatoes, sliced or chopped
1 ripe avocado, sliced or chopped
1 sweet onion, sliced or chopped
1 cucumber, thinly sliced
Dolphin Salad (see page 56)

   1. Combine flour, salt and water in mixing bowl. Use more water as needed to make mixture moist yet not sticky.
   2. Mold into two-inch round, flat patties, like hamburgers, and set aside 5 minutes.
   3. Preheat oven to 350°F.
   4. Over medium-high heat, warm a heavy skillet coated with Pam, olive oil or butter and lightly brown each side of the arepas.
   5. Place on cookie sheet and bake 15 to 20 minutes. Serve hot with garnishes. The arepas can be used as a cracker or sliced in half like a hamburger bun and stuffed. Many people like to remove the insidemeat and simply use the remaining shell to contain the filling.

Makes 8 to 10 arepas.

*Found in Spanish-American food markets.

POTATO PANCAKES WITH CAVIAR

1 medium to large potato
1 small onion
1 egg, beaten
1½ tablespoons flour
1 heaping tablespoon fresh dill, chopped
pinch baking powder
salt and freshly ground pepper to taste
¼ cup vegetable oil
1 pint sour cream (use as needed)
1 can (4 ounces) black or red caviar (use as needed)

1. Grate potato and onion. Drain well.

2. Add beaten egg, flour, dill, baking powder, salt and fresh pepper.

3. Heat oil in a skillet. Drop heaping spoonfuls of batter into hot oil, one at a time. Fry until golden brown on both sides, about 1½ minutes each side.

4. Put a dollop of sour cream and 1 teaspoon caviar on each pancake and serve immediately.

Serves 2.

ANNE TANNENBAUM'S
SWEET 'N SOUR MEATBALLS

2 pounds ground beef
1 slice bread, moistened with milk
2 eggs
salt and pepper to taste
2 tablespoons vegetable oil
2 medium onions, diced
1 clove garlic
1 bottle (12 ounces) Heinz chili sauce
1 bottle (12 ounces) water (use chili sauce bottle)
1 10-ounce jar grape jelly

1. Combine sirloin, bread, eggs, salt and pepper. Form into 1 inch meatballs and set aside.

2. In large skillet sauté onions and garlic in oil over moderately low heat. Increase heat to medium and brown meatballs.

3. In large saucepan heat chili sauce, water and jelly; bring to boiling point. Add meatballs to sauce and simmer aprroximately one hour.

Serves 6.

ISLAND COCONUT SHRIMP

30 large raw shrimp, peeled and deveined
1/2 cup all-purpose flour
1/4 cup bread crumbs
3 eggs, beaten
4 cups shredded coconut
vegetable oil for frying

Honey Mustard Sauce:
3/4 cup mustard
1/2 cup honey

1. Combine flour and bread crumbs. Dredge shrimp in flour mixture, then beaten eggs. Roll shrimp through shredded coconut, covering them thoroughly.
2. Deep-fry shrimp at about 375°F. or heat oil until a haze appears and cook shrimp until brown.
3. Mix mustard and honey together and adjust to taste. Serve shrimp with honey mustard sauce on side.

Serves 6.

GRILLED SHRIMP WITH CILANTRO

For those who love shrimp, this is simple, elegant and flavorful.

2 jalapeño peppers
2 large tomatoes, seeded (see page 95)
1 large bunch cilantro leaves, chopped
salt and pepper to taste
3 1/2 pounds jumbo shrimp
1 1/2 cups butter
2 cloves garlic, finely minced
4 limes

1. Seed and mince peppers. Seed and chop tomato. Chop cilantro. Mix 3/4 cup cilantro with tomato and season to taste with salt and pepper.
2. Peel and devein shrimp.
3. Heat broiler. Melt butter in saucepan. Add jalapeño pepper, garlic and 1/4 cup cilantro. Squeeze in juice from limes and season with salt and pepper.
4. Brush shrimp with some of melted butter mixture. Broil shrimp until it tests done, about 2 minutes total. To serve, put remaining butter sauce on each plate, top with 5 shrimp and a dollop of tomato mixture in the center.

Serves 6 to 8.

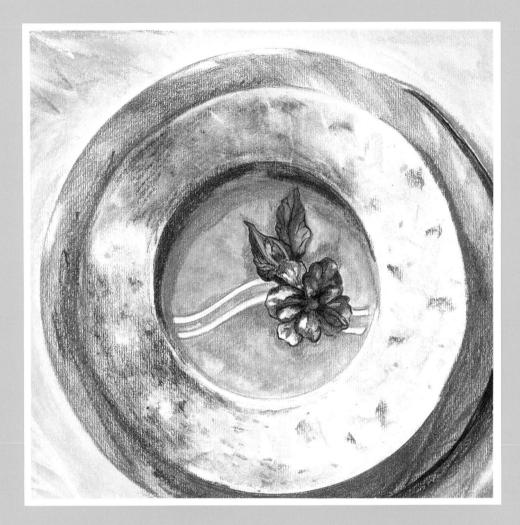

Soups

PEPPERY LENTIL SOUP

5 tablespoons olive oil
3 medium onions, chopped
½ teaspoon salt
2 cloves garlic, minced
1½ teaspoons ground cumin, or to taste
1½ cups dry lentils
1 teaspoon oregano
1 teaspoon paprika
¾ teaspoon cayenne
1 quart water
1 can (28 ounces) plum tomatoes, chopped
salt and black pepper to taste
3 cups beef broth
½ cup sour cream
fresh cilantro leaves, chopped, for garnish

1. Heat oil in large pot. Add onions, sprinkle with ½ teaspoon salt and cook over low heat until soft, about 3 minutes. Add garlic and cook 30 seconds. Stir in cumin and cook about 2 minutes, until lightly toasted. Add lentils, oregano, paprika, and cayenne and stir to coat with oil. Add water and tomatoes and bring to a simmer.

2. Lower heat, season with salt and pepper and cook, covered, until lentils are soft but not mushy, about 30 minutes.

3. Add 1½ cups beef broth. Simmer 30 minutes.

4. Add remaining 1½ cups beef broth; let simmer another 30 minutes.

5. Adjust seasonings to taste.

6. Serve with a dollop of sour cream and sprinkle with cilantro leaves.

Serves 6 to 8.

GAZPACHO PERFECTO

A marvelous summer soup or even a vegetable drink to keep you cool and nourished in the heat of the summer. Serve very cold.

1 clove garlic, minced
1 medium onion, sliced
1 cucumber, sliced
3 tomatoes, peeled (see page 95)
1 green pepper, seeded and diced
1 red pepper, seeded and diced
¼ cup red wine vinegar
¼ cup olive oil
¾ cup tomato juice
salt, pepper and Tabasco to taste
1 tablespoon key lime juice

   1. In blender or food processor combine garlic, onion, cucumber, tomatoes, green and red peppers. Add vinegar, olive oil, tomato juice, key lime juice, salt, pepper and Tabasco and blend again. Don't quite purée.
   2. Chill and serve with garnishes on the side.

Serves 6.

Garnishes served in individual bowls:

1 cup croutons
1 cucumber, diced
1 onion, chopped
1 green pepper, seeded and chopped
1 tomato, chopped

CHICKEN BROTH

The cooked chicken is ideal for Jackie's Cashew Chicken Salad or Chicken Pot Pie. We also suggest that if you're feeling low or running a fever you put the chicken in the broth, heat, eat and feel better!

2 chickens – 3 pounds each, cut up
4 quarts water
6 carrots, sliced
4 stalks celery with leaves, chopped
2 parsnips, cubed
4 onions, sliced
2 leeks, white part only, quartered
bouquet garni (bay leaf, parsley, thyme wrapped in cheesecloth)
2 sprigs fresh dill or 1 teasoon dry dill weed
juice of one lemon
2 cloves garlic, whole
3 peppercorns
½ teaspoon ground ginger

1. Put chicken in an 8 to 10 quart pot and add water to cover. Bring to a low boil and skim off froth with a large, slotted mesh spoon.

2. Add remaining ingredients and again bring to a low boil. Skim again. Reduce heat and simmer, covered, 3 to 6 hours. Refrigerate meat. Remove chicken when tender, after approximately 1 hour; discard skin.

3. Strain contents through a fine sieve or colander lined with cheesecloth, placed over a large bowl. Let cool, refrigerate and remove hardened fat from top.

Makes four quarts.

This broth can be refrigerated 5 to 6 days or frozen (in 1 or 2 cup portions), up to 2 months. Boil frozen broth before using and season to taste with salt at that time. Use cooked chicken within 1 to 2 days or freeze.

MEAT BROTH

The boiled meat may be served simply with horseradish, in a "Sofrito" sauce, on Arepas or Marvelous Mashed Potatoes with your choice of sauce. The broth makes delicious Onion Soup.

2 pounds beef shank
2 pounds beef short ribs
2 pounds chicken pieces (backs, necks, wings)
1 veal shank or 2 pounds veal bones and knuckle quarters,
*   cut crosswise*
¼ cup olive oil (optional)
5 quarts water
8 carrots, sliced
4 stalks celery with leaves, chopped
4 medium onions
4 whole cloves (one stuck in each onion)
2 leeks, white part only, quartered
bouquet garni (bay leaf, parsley, thyme wrapped in cheesecloth)
2 cloves garlic, whole
*juice of one lemon or 3 tomatoes, quartered

1. Brown meat either in a 450°F. oven for 30 to 40 minutes or in hot oil in a large stock pot over medium-high heat.

2. In stock pot add water to bones and meat and bring slowly just to the boiling point; skim with a mesh or slotted spoon to remove froth that rises to the surface.

3. Add remaining ingredients, bring to slow boil again and skim once more before reducing heat to simmer. Simmer partially covered, approximately 5 hours.

4. Strain entire contents through a fine sieve or colander lined with cheesecloth, placed over a large bowl. Let cool, refrigerate and remove hardened fat from top.

Makes 4 quarts.

*Either may be used for acidity to extract flavor and calcium from bones.

This broth can be refrigerated 5 to 6 days or frozen (in 1 or 2 cup portions), up to 2 months. Boil frozen broth before using and season to taste with salt at that time.

BISCAYNE BAY FISH BROTH

The beginning of a delicious, nutritious fish soup; or use for poaching fish.

2 pounds fish trimmings: heads, tails and bones of any firm,
*   white-fleshed fish*
¼ cup olive oil
2 tablespoons butter
2 carrots, sliced
1 large onion, sliced
2 shallots, chopped
1 stalk celery with leaves, chopped
*¼ cup fresh lime juice or 1 tomato, diced
1¼ cups dry white wine
bouquet garni (bay leaf, parsley and thyme wrapped in cheesecloth)
cold water
salt and pepper to taste

   1. Rinse fish trimmings under cold water.
   2. Heat oil in heavy, four quart stock pot over medium-high heat and sauté fish trimmings, stirring about 10 minutes.
   3. Lower heat to medium. Add butter, carrots, onions, shallots and celery. Cook another 5 minutes.
   4. Stir in lime juice or tomatoes, then wine and simmer until most of the moisture evaporates.
   5. Add bouquet garni, and enough cold water to cover.
   6. Bring to a boil over high heat. With a large, mesh or slotted spoon, skim off froth that rises to surface. Reduce to low heat, cover and simmer 30 minutes; skim occasionally.
   7. Strain entire contents through a fine sieve or colander lined with cheesecloth, placed over a large bowl. Press lightly with back of spoon to extract as much liquid as possible before discarding solid ingredients.
   8. Let cool, refrigerate and remove hardened fat from top.

Makes 4 quarts.

*Either may be used for acidity to extract flavor and calcium from bones.

This broth can be refrigerated 2 to 3 days or frozen (in 1 or 2 cup portions), up to 6 weeks. Boil frozen broth before using and season to taste.

VENEZUELAN FISH SOUP

Robert and Marisela Gross introduced Bev's family to a varietal fish soup while visiting Venezuela. They serve it with Arepas and garnishes for a relaxing dinner party and "Bolas Criollas" tournament. This is Bev's combination of that "Sancocho" and a "Bouillabaisse" she and her husband enjoyed in Beaulieu-sur-Mer.

2 pounds king fish or grouper, cut into two-inch chunks
1 tablespoon Creole Seasoning (see page 87)
4 tablespoons olive oil
2 medium onions, slivered
2 cloves garlic, crushed
*2 cups calabaza, chopped (substitute pumpkin or other hard
*   squash, cubed)*
*2 cups malanga, chopped (substitute potatoes, cubed)
1 bay leaf
black pepper to taste
pinch cayenne pepper
½ teaspoon oregano
1 tablespoon ground coriander
1 cup dry white wine
4 cups fish broth, boiling (see page 34)
1 can (12 ounces) whole tomatoes, undrained and puréed
lime wedges for garnish
French bread, thinly sliced and toasted
1 recipe Alex's Alioli Sauce (see page 115)
Parmesan cheese, grated

1. Rinse fish and pat dry with paper towels. Sprinkle with creole seasoning; set aside and keep cool.

2. In large soup pot, sauté onions and garlic in olive oil until soft. Add remaining ingredients, except fish, and bring to a boil. Lower heat and simmer 30 minutes or until vegetables are tender.

3. Ten minutes before serving, return soup to a boil. Add fish chunks and cook until fish is heated through. Garnish with lime or lemon wedges. Serve with toasted French bread circles topped with Alex's Alioli Sauce and Parmesan cheese.

Serves 4.

*Calabaza and malanga can be found in Spanish-American markets, if not in most grocery stores.

POTATO SOUP WITH KALE AND BACON

3½ pounds red potatoes
water
2 pounds bacon
1½ pounds kale, stemmed and chopped
1½ cloves garlic, minced
salt and pepper to taste
1¾ cups heavy cream
¾ cup chicken broth
5 teaspoons balsamic vinegar
1 bunch chives, minced

1. Peel potatoes and put in large pot with cold, salted water to cover. Cover and bring to a boil. Lower heat to a simmer, uncover and cook until done, about 25 minutes. Drain, reserving cooking liquid. Mash potatoes with a potato masher; they should be lumpy, not smooth.

2. Meanwhile, cook bacon until crisp; drain and chop. Pour off all but 2 tablespoons bacon fat, reserving excess.

3. Add half the kale and half the garlic to frying pan. Season with salt and pepper and cook over medium heat until kale is wilted, about 1 minute. Transfer to a bowl. Repeat with remaining garlic and kale. Use remaining bacon fat as needed. Return all kale to frying pan and add heavy cream.

4. Simmer over low heat until kale is tender, about 10 minutes.

5. Combine potatoes with about 3½ cups of reserved cooking liquid. Add chicken broth and kale mixture.

6. Return to frying pan and bring to a simmer. Season to taste with vinegar, salt and pepper. Pour soup into individual bowls. Sprinkle with chives and bacon.

Serves 6 to 8.

CHILLED AVOCADO SOUP WITH VODKA

This is a wonderful summer buffet starter.

3 to 4 large, ripe avocados
3 cups chicken broth, cooled
½ cup vodka
1 tablespoon lemon juice
½ cup sweet or sour cream (or a combination of both)
a few drops of Tabasco sauce to taste
salt and pepper to taste

1. Purée avocados in either a blender or food processor. Add a bit of chicken broth to aid the puréeing.
2. When very smooth add to chicken broth. Stir in vodka, lemon juice, cream, Tabasco, salt and pepper.
3. Chill and serve with garnishes.

Garnishes served in individual bowls:
2 large tomatoes, chopped
2 cucumbers, diced
2 onions, chopped
2 green peppers, chopped
2 red peppers, chopped
1 bowl cheese tortilla chips

Serves 4.

WARM AVOCADO SOUP

2 large or 3 small ripe avocados
3 cups chicken broth
2 cups half and half cream
salt to taste
freshly ground pepper, preferably white, to taste

Garnishes:
1 tablespoon fresh cilantro, finely chopped
croutons or fried tortillas (optional)

1. Heat broth and cream.
2. Peel avocados, mash through a sieve, and put into heated serving tureen or bowl.
3. Whisk warm broth into mashed avocados.
4. Season to taste with salt and pepper.
5. Garnish with cilantro and serve immediately with croutons or fried tortillas.

Serves 4.

BELLE ISLE YOGURT SOUP

4½ cups yogurt
1 tablespoon heavy cream
¾ cup water
4 cucumbers, peeled and coarsely grated
1 teaspoon fresh dill, chopped
juice of ½ lemon or key lime
1 tablespoon raisins (or currants)
½ teaspoon salt
⅓ cup almonds, ground

1. Mix yogurt, cream and water.
2. Add cucumbers, dill, lemon juice, raisins and salt.
3. Sprinkle almonds over top. Serve chilled.

Serves 4 or 5.

BRANDIED BROCCOLI SOUP WITH PEARS

1 bunch fresh broccoli
3 tablespoons butter
1 small onion, thinly sliced
1 pear, peeled, cored and diced
½ cup brandy
3½ cups chicken broth
salt and pepper to taste
2 tablespoons chives, minced

1. Cut broccoli into small pieces.
2. Melt butter in soup kettle. Add onions, pear and brandy. Cover and cook over low heat 10 minutes.
3. Add broccoli, chicken broth, salt and pepper. Bring to a boil and simmer, covered, over medium heat 30 minutes.
4. Remove soup from heat, cool and blend in blender or food processor until smooth.
5. Reheat soup. Sprinkle with chives and serve.

Serves 4.

ICED CUCUMBER SOUP

3 cups cucumber, peeled and chopped
1 clove garlic, minced
4 cups sour cream
1 cup milk
½ cup heavy cream
1 cup fresh chives, chopped
¾ cup fresh parsley, chopped
1½ tablespoons fresh dill, minced
¼ teaspoon nutmeg (optional)

1. Place cucumbers and garlic in stainless steel bowl. Add sour cream and mix gently.
2. Slowly add milk and cream until well blended.
3. Blend in chives, parsley, dill and nutmeg (if desired). Serve in chilled soup cups.

Serves 6 to 8.

CONSOMMÉ ROUGE

2 medium onions, sliced paper thin
water
3 small beets, peeled and grated
1 teaspoon salt
3 teaspoons red wine
1½ quarts rich chicken broth (skimmed of all fat)

1. In large saucepan, cook onions in water to cover until soft.
2. Pour off liquid, grate beets into saucepan, add salt, wine and chicken broth.
3. Bring to a boil, reduce heat and simmer, uncovered, 30 minutes. Remove from heat, strain vegetables and set aside. Serve consommé as is or place small amount of onion and beets in individual serving bowls and pour in consommé.

Serves 6 to 8.

DIANE'S "FULL OF BEANS" SOUP

This is an all day soup with a hearty, lingering aroma – contributed by Jackie's sister, Diane.

2 cups combination of beans, such as peas, lentils, black beans, northern beans, navy beans, chick peas, lima beans and barley. (Always include at least 2 tablespoons barley for thickener).
water
6 cups chicken broth
liquid from soaking beans
1¾ cups Burgundy wine
3 leeks, chopped
2 parsnips, chopped
2 cloves garlic, crushed
1 bay leaf
½ tablespoon each, of: fresh parsley, oregano, thyme and basil, chopped
2 tomatoes, cut in pieces
¼ eggplant, peeled and diced
1 potato, diced (for very thick soup)
1 green pepper, chopped
salt, pepper and paprika to taste
2 tablespoons all-purpose flour (optional)
additional Burgundy wine (optional)

1. Cover beans with water and soak overnight.

2. Next day, drain beans and reserve liquid.

3. In large soup pot combine reserved liquid with chicken broth and Burgundy wine to make 10 cups liquid.

4. Add beans and remaining ingredients including salt, pepper and paprika.

5. Simmer on low heat until beans are cooked, at least 6 to 8 hours.

6. If the soup isn't thick enough, mix in 2 tablespoons flour. If too thick, add additional Burgundy.

Serves 8.

LITTLE HAVANA BLACK BEAN SOUP

1½ pounds black beans
2¼ quarts water (9 cups)
1 tablespoon plus 1 teaspoon salt
3 to 5 cloves garlic, minced
1 teaspoon ground cumin
1 teaspoon oregano
¼ teaspoon dry mustard
3 tablespoons olive oil
2 onions, chopped
1 green pepper, chopped
1 tablespoon fresh lemon juice
⅓ cup white wine (optional)

Garnishes:
cooked rice
scallion greens, chopped
onions, diced
hard-boiled eggs, diced

1. Soak beans in water overnight. Next day, using same water, add 1 tablespoon salt and bring to a boil. Cover and cook until beans are almost tender, approximately 1½ to 2 hours.

2. Mix together garlic, 1 teaspoon salt, cumin, oregano, and dry mustard.

3. In large skillet heat oil and sauté onions, about 5 minutes. Add green pepper and continue sautéing until onions are tender. Stir in seasoning mixture, lemon juice, wine (if desired), then about ½ cup of the hot bean liquid. Cover and simmer about 10 minutes. Add to beans and continue cooking until flavors are thoroughly blended, approximately 1 hour.

4. To thicken soup, remove 1 cup of beans and liquid and put through an electric blender. Return purée to soup pot.

5. Serve in bowls with rice in center. Garnish with scallions, raw onions or diced hard-boiled eggs.

Serves 8 to 10.

ONION SOUP

7 cups sweet onions (Vidalia, if possible), thinly sliced
½ cup butter
3 tablespoons all-purpose flour
7 cups beef broth, boiling
½ teaspoon pepper
6 to 8 ounces Gruyere or swiss cheese, thinly sliced
12 slices french bread, toasted
Parmesan cheese, grated

1. Slowly sauté onions in butter over low heat in large, covered saucepan 15 to 20 minutes; stir occasionally.

2. Add flour and mix five minutes or until smooth.

3. Stirring constantly, add broth and pepper. Cover and cook 30 minutes over low heat. (Can be made to this point a day or two in advance, but reheat before pouring into serving bowls).

4. Preheat oven to 350°F. Cover bottom of each oven-proof soup bowl with pieces of cheese; pour in soup. Top with bread slices and sprinkle with Parmesan cheese.

5. Bake 5 to 10 minutes; place under broiler 1 to 2 minutes to brown.

Serves 6.

Salads

LINCOLN ROAD SPINACH SALAD

1½ pounds fresh spinach
½ pound mushrooms, thinly sliced
4 hard-boiled eggs, sliced
½ cup vegetable or safflower oil
1 teaspoon sesame oil
2 teaspoons sugar
5 tablespoons lemon juice
1 teaspoon honey
1¼ teaspoons Dijon mustard
freshly ground black pepper
8 strips bacon, fried crisp, drained and crumbled

1. Wash and dry spinach. Discard stems and tear leaves into bite-sized pieces. Toss spinach, mushrooms and egg together in salad bowl.
2. In separate bowl whisk together vegetable or safflower oil, sesame oil, sugar, lemon juice, honey, mustard and pepper.
3. Pour over salad and toss until all leaves are coated. Serve on individual plates and sprinkle bacon over each serving.

Serves 6.

JACKIE'S CASHEW CHICKEN SALAD

This recipe utilizes the leftover chicken when making chicken broth.

1 cup chicken, boiled, skinned and cooled
1 apple, unpeeled
2 stalks celery
¼ cup cashews
salt and pepper to taste
¼ teaspoon curry
1 tablespoon fresh dill, chopped
¼ cup mayonnaise

1. Cut chicken, cored apple and celery into bite-size pieces and combine in bowl.
2. Add cashews, salt, pepper, curry, dill and mayonnaise and mix well.
3. Chill before serving.

Serves 2.

CHINESE CHICKEN SALAD

This recipe takes time, but is well worth your while.

vegetable oil for deep frying
*2 ounces cellophane noodles
1 teaspoon vegetable oil
2 eggs, each lightly beaten, separately
3½ cups cooked chicken, shredded
½ head iceberg or Chinese lettuce, shredded
1 carrot, shredded
½ cup scallions, chopped
*5 tablespoons Hoisin sauce
*3 tablespoons rice wine vinegar
1 tablespoon granulated sugar
1 tablespoon soy sauce
1 tablespoon sesame oil
1 cup stir-fried cashews or walnuts (optional)

1. In wok or deep skillet heat 1 inch of oil to 400°F, or until it begins to smoke. Add one quarter of noodles and fry, turning once, until puffed, about 5 seconds. Drain on paper towels. Repeat with remaining noodles.

2. Wipe wok or skillet and heat until water sprinkled on surface beads. Add 1 teaspoon oil and tilt to coat bottom. Add one egg and tilt to coat as for an omelet. Cook, turning once, until firm, about 10 seconds. Transfer to plate and cut into thin strips. Repeat with second egg.

3. In large bowl, combine chicken, lettuce, carrot, scallions and egg strips. In small bowl, combine Hoisin sauce, vinegar, sugar, soy sauce and sesame oil. Pour over salad, add noodles and toss. If desired add cashews or walnuts.

Serves 6 to 8.

*Found in oriental groceries or in specialty section of supermarket.

ELKA'S POTATO SALAD

This salad is great with Blackie's barbeque chicken or hamburgers.

4 potatoes, peeled
4 hard-boiled eggs, cooled and peeled
2 cucumbers, peeled chopped or 1 medium onion, chopped
2 tablespoons fresh dill, chopped
2 tablespoons fresh chives, chopped
1 cup mayonnaise, or more to taste
salt and freshly ground pepper to taste
2 tablespoons white vinegar
paprika

1. Boil potatoes until tender and cool.
2. Cut potatoes and eggs into pieces. Add cucumbers or onion, dill, chives, salt, pepper, mayonnaise and vinegar. Mix well.
3. Sprinkle with paprika and refrigerate a few hours before serving.

Serves 6.

GINGER'S POTATO SALAD

5 pounds new red potatoes, unpeeled
1 small Vidalia or red onion, minced
1 small red pepper, finely chopped
1 small green pepper, finely chopped
¾ pound bacon, cooked crisp and crumbled
2 hard-boiled eggs, grated
1 carrot, finely shredded
1½ cups mayonnaise
2 tablespoons Dijon mustard
1 tablespoon black pepper, coarsely ground
1 to 2 teaspoons celery salt to taste
pinch cayenne pepper
1 teaspoon white vinegar, as needed

1. Cook potatoes until soft, either in boiling water 20 to 30 minutes or in microwave 10 to 12 minutes. Let cool, cut into large chunks and set aside until thoroughly cooled.
2. Combine remaining ingredients and toss with potatoes.

Serves approximately 20.

KAY'S POTATO SALAD

Bev's mom's traditional potato salad has become our favorite.

*8 cups white potatoes, cooked and diced
   (approximately 8 medium potatoes)
2½ cups onions, diced
8 hard-boiled eggs
*4 large carrots, shredded
1½ teaspoons salt
¼ teaspoon pepper
1½ cups mayonnaise
paprika for garnish*

    1. While still warm, add potatoes to onions in large bowl. Mix well and set aside to cool.

    2. Separate hard-boiled egg whites from yolks and set yolks aside for garnish. Dice whites and add to potatoes along with carrot shreds, salt and pepper. Mix in mayonnaise.

    3. Mound salad on serving platter and garnish with 3 to 4 egg yolks pushed through a strainer with the back of a spoon. Sprinkle with paprika.

Serves 10 to 12.

*Bev's mother curiously scraped the carrots for this potato salad. To do this, use the wrong edge of a knife to first scrape off the outer brown layer of skin and discard. Continue to scrape carrots in this manner to extract the sweetness and color of the carrots and let scrapings fall into salad. When core is reached, place in cold water and eat as a snack.

DUCK KEY CURRIED PASTA SALAD

This salad is a good informal party food, especially when friends can help cut, dice and participate. It keeps well for several days.

Dressing:
1 cup mayonnaise
2 cloves garlic, crushed
¼ cup rice wine vinegar
2 teaspoons curry powder
¼ cup combination of fresh herbs, chopped (such as: basil, thyme,
  rosemary, parsley)

Other Ingredients:
3 cups combination of fresh vegetables, for steaming; cut into bite-sized
  pieces (such as: zucchini, squash, carrots, green beans, broccoli,
  peas, asparagus, corn, brussel sprouts, cauliflower)
1 cup combination of fresh vegetables, diced (such as: red cabbage,
  sweet red, green or yellow peppers, scallions)
8 ounces pasta twists
½ cup onions, diced
1½ cups chicken, cooked and cubed
¼ cup sandwich pepperoni, diced

Choice of toppings for garnish:
Alfafa sprouts, cucumbers, cherry tomatoes, Feta cheese, olives, red cabbage, snow peas.

1. Make dressing a day in advance, if you wish, by mixing mayonnaise, garlic, vinegar, curry and herbs. Refrigerate.

2. Cut 2 cups choice of vegetables to be steamed. Set aside.

3. Dice 1 cup of uncooked vegetables. Set aside.

4. Cook pasta al dente and add onions while pasta is still hot. Steam vegetables lightly and mix together with pasta. Add diced, uncooked ingredients and mix again. Work in sauce and mix well.

5. Transfer to large salad or serving bowl and garnish in circular pattern with choice of colorful toppings. Serve immediately or refrigerate and serve cold.

Serves 8.

CLASSIC ISRAELI SALAD

2 green peppers, finely chopped
2 red peppers, finely chopped
1 avocado, finely chopped
2 tomatoes, finely chopped
2 cucumbers, finely chopped
3 carrots (medium to large), finely chopped
salt and pepper to taste
juice of one lemon

1. Toss together all the vegetables with salt, pepper and lemon juice. Chill and serve.

Serves 4.

TABBOULEH

2 cups fine bulghur (crushed wheat)
cold water to cover
1 large onion, finely chopped
½ cup scallions, finely chopped
salt and pepper to taste
2 cups fresh parsley, finely chopped
4 tablespoons fresh mint, finely chopped or 2 tablespoons dried
1½ teaspoons allspice
½ cup olive oil
¾ cup lemon juice
2 ripe tomatoes, chopped (optional)

1. Soak bulghur in cold water for ½ hour. The water should cover the bulghur. Drain as dry as possible and squeeze with hands to remove excess moisture.

2. Add onions, scallions, salt, pepper, parsley, mint, allspice, oil, lemon juice and tomatoes. Mix well and let set in refrigerator at least 3 hours before serving.

Serves 4.

DOLPHIN SALAD SUPREME

4½ to 5 pounds fresh dolphin fillets (approximately 7 cups cooked
  dolphin, flaked)
2 cups or more water to cover
1 tablespoon oregano
1 tablespoon thyme
juice of one lemon

Salad Ingredients:
7 cups cooked dolphin, flaked
1¼ cups onions, finely chopped
2 cups celery, diced
1 cup green pepper, diced
1 cup red pepper, diced
juice of one lime
¾ teaspoon ground thyme
½ cup scallions, chopped
¼ teaspoon freshly ground pepper, or to taste
1½ cups mayonnaise
leafy lettuce
alfalfa sprouts, paprika, and cherry tomatoes for garnish

1. In a large pot bring aproximately 3 inches water to a boil. Add oregano, thyme, lemon juice and fish, one fillet at a time. Try to maintain a full boil. Cook each fillet approximately 3 minutes and remove when fish flakes easily, when tested with a fork.

2. Drain fillets, place in large mixing bowl, and flake with a fork. Stir in onions while fish is still hot.

3. Add celery, green and red peppers, lime juice, ground thyme, scallions and pepper. Mix well. Stir in mayonnaise and taste to adjust seasonings.

4. Serve on a large platter lined with green leafy lettuce, surrounded with alfalfa sprouts and cherry tomatoes, and sprinkled with paprika.

Serves approximately 20 sandwich portions.

LILLY'S LOBSTER SALAD

A light, beautiful, rich lobster salad for a lazy summer afternoon.

4 cups cooked lobster
¾ cup celery, chopped
½ cup mayonnaise
¼ cup whipped cream
½ teaspoon curry
1 head bibb lettuce
fresh parsley, chopped
1 hard-boiled egg, grated

1. Cut lobster meat into bite-size pieces, place in bowl and add celery.

2. Blend mayonnaise, whipped cream and curry in separate small bowl, then gently combine with lobster.

3. Arrange a bed of lettuce leaves on serving platter and put lobster salad on top. Garnish with parsley and egg.

Serves 8.

WALNUT SALAD SURPRISE

1 head bibb lettuce
½ Radicchio
4 spears Belgian endive
¾ cup walnut oil
¼ cup red wine vinegar
2 tablespoons Dijon mustard
salt and freshly ground pepper to taste
4 ounces Montrachet goat cheese rolled in chopped dill, basil, chives
*   and parsley*
1 ripe pear or mango
¼ cup walnuts, chopped

1. Wash and dry lettuce, radicchio and endive and arrange on a salad plate.

2. Whisk together oil, vinegar, mustard, salt and pepper and set aside.

3. Cut herb-wrapped goat cheese into small pieces.

4. Just before serving, slice pear or mango and top salad with fruit, goat cheese, dressing and walnuts.

Serves 4.

TO THE
BACKRO

THE
MUSIC ROOM

804 OCEAN DRIVE

BILTMORE WAY CAESAR SALAD

1 head crisp, fresh romaine lettuce
2 cloves garlic, crushed
freshly ground pepper
1 egg yolk
½ teaspoon Worcestershire sauce
1 tablespoon Dijon mustard
⅛ teaspoon Tabasco
1 teaspoon fresh lemon juice
¼ cup fresh croutons (optional)
¼ cup Parmesan cheese, grated; additional for serving
up to 1 tablespoon olive oil (optional)

1. Wash and dry romaine; break into pieces and chill.

2. Coat wooden salad bowl well with garlic. Remove most of the garlic pieces and save for fresh croutons, garlic bread or discard.

3. Lightly coat bowl with pepper; add egg yolk, Worcestershire sauce, mustard, Tabasco and lemon juice. Mix well and rotate the bowl to evenly coat with dressing. Salad can be prepared to this point up to 1 hour in advance.

4. To make fresh croutons, preheat oven to 350°F, lightly butter sliced french bread, coat with extra garlic and cut into cubes. Place one layer deep on cookie sheet and bake until brown, approximately 10 minutes. Turn frequently.

5. Just before serving, toss romaine with dressing, Parmesan cheese and croutons. Crush a few of the croutons against sides of bowl. Add a little olive oil at this point only if the salad is dry. Place on two salad plates; pass peppermill and additional Parmesan cheese.

Serves 2.

HEARTS OF PALM, ARTICHOKE AND SHRIMP SALAD

4 heads bibb lettuce, cleaned and dried
2 pounds mushrooms, thinly sliced
2 cans (14 ounces each) hearts of palm, drained and diced
2 avocados, peeled and sliced
2 cups crisp bacon, crumbled (about 12 slices)
1 can (14 ounces) artichoke hearts, drained and cut in small pieces
2 pounds shrimp, peeled, deveined, cooked and cooled
*   (reserve 6 for garnish) or stone crab substitute.*
4 hard boiled eggs, grated, as garnish
bunch parsley, finely chopped, as garnish

Dressing:
1½ cups vegetable oil
½ cup red wine vinegar
juice of one lemon
2 cloves garlic, minced
1 teaspoon Worcestershire sauce
2 tablespoons chili sauce
1½ tablespoons Coleman's Hot English mustard
5 tablespoons Parmesan cheese, grated
fresh ground pepper to taste

1. Lightly toss all salad ingredients, except garnishes.
2. Blend together salad dressing ingredients.
3. Toss salad with dressing. Garnish with shrimp, egg and parsley.

Serves 8.

Vegetables
Rice & Pasta

CHAMPAGNE CABBAGE

¼ cup butter
2 large onions, thinly sliced
3 large Granny Smith apples, pared, cored, and cut into
    ⅛-inch thick slices
1 small red cabbage (about 1 pound), thinly sliced
1 small green cabbage (about 1 pound), thinly sliced
1½ cups champagne, room temperature
2 tablespoons granulated sugar
1 tablespoon lemon juice
1 tablespoon lime juice
1 teaspoon salt
¼ teaspoon freshly ground pepper
⅛ teaspoon nutmeg
¾ cup golden raisins (optional)

1. Heat butter in large Dutch oven or heavy pot. Add onions and sauté, stirring often until golden brown, about 8 minutes.

2. Add apples, sauté 5 minutes, and reduce heat.

3. Add cabbages, ½ cup champagne, sugar, lemon and lime juice, salt, pepper and nutmeg. Add raisins if desired. Cook, covered, for 20 minutes. Add remaining champagne and cook, uncovered, for 10 minutes.

4. Transfer to a serving dish and serve.

Serves 8 to 10.

DEEP-FRIED SAUERKRAUT BALLS

1 large (about ½ pound) white potato, peeled and cut
    into ¾ inch cubes
1 teaspoon unsalted butter
¼ cup half-and-half (half milk, half cream)
salt and pepper to taste
12 ounces sauerkraut, rinsed, squeezed dry, and fluffed lightly
    (about 1½ cups)
1 teaspoon Dijon mustard
½ cup cooked ham, minced
½ cup ground sausage meat (see page 128)
½ cup parsely, minced
2 scallions, minced
1 egg
1 tablespoon water
2 cups fresh bread crumbs
¼ cup Parmesan cheese
vegetable oil for deep-frying

1. In saucepan boil potato 15 minutes, or until very tender. Drain potatoes and using a fork mash with butter, cream, salt and pepper to taste, until mixture is smooth. Stir in sauerkraut, mustard, ham, sausage, parsley and scallions.

2. With floured hands, roll mixture into 1½ inch balls. Chill 2 hours.

3. Beat together the egg and 1 tablespoon water. Dip balls in egg wash, then roll in the bread crumbs mixed with Parmesan cheese.

4. In a deep fryer heat 3 inches vegetable oil to 350°F., or until a haze appears. Fry the balls in batches in hot oil 2 mintues, or until golden, transferring with a slotted spoon to paper towels to drain as they are fried.

Makes 24 balls.

BLACK BEANS

After returning from Venezuela, Bev wanted to duplicate the "Domino Arepas" (black beans and white cheese) found on nearly every corner restaurant there. Jesus, formerly from La Parisien Supermarket on Miami Beach, introduced her to "aji cachucha" and this recipe.

*6 ounces dried black beans, rinsed
water
1½ medium green peppers
2 medium onions
1 clove garlic, minced
**2 aji cachucha, minced*

1. In medium saucepan, add beans and water to cover 1 inch beyond top of beans. Add ½ green pepper, deribbed, and 1 whole onion, peeled. Bring to boil, reduce heat and simmer approximately 2 hours or until beans are soft.

2. In another saucepan heat oil over medium high heat, add ½ green pepper, chopped and sauté 5 minutes. Add remaining onion, chopped, the garlic and aji cachucha; sauté another 5 minutes, stirring occasionally.

3. Add beans and liquid, bring to a boil, reduce heat and simmer at least 15 minutes.

4. Ten minutes before serving, remove from heat, add remaining green pepper half, uncut, to beans for aromatics.

Makes 2¼ cups.

*Substitute a 15 ounce can black beans.
**Found in Spanish food markets. It is a small sweet bonnet pepper.

PEARLIZED ONIONS

1 pint pearl onions
water for cooking
¼ teaspoon salt
freshly ground pepper to taste
⅛ teaspoon ground ginger
2 tablespoons butter, cut into bits

1. In medium saucepan cover whole unpeeled onions with water and bring to a boil for two to three minutes. Remove from heat, drain and let cool enough to handle. To peel, cut off root end and squeeze onion through stem end.

2. Preheat oven to 350°F.

3. Place peeled onions one layer deep in baking dish. Sprinkle with salt, pepper and ginger. Dot with butter.

4. Bake 30 minutes covered with aluminum foil, then 10 minutes uncovered. Serve as a condiment with Roasted Holiday Turkey.

Makes 1 pint.

BEET AND CARROT PURÉE

This adds wonderful color to any meal!

3 beets, peeled and sliced
1½ pounds carrots, pared and sliced
water to cover
4 tablespoons butter
1 teaspoon fresh lemon juice (optional)
1 teaspoon dill weed

1. Cook beets and carrots separately until tender in water to cover. Drain and set aside, reserving the liquids.

2. Purée beets and carrots in a food processor or blender. Add just enough of the reserved liquids to obtain a smooth texture.

3. Add butter, lemon juice, if desired, and dill weed; process a few seconds more. Keep warm in a double boiler.

Serves 4.

RATATOUILLE

⅓ cup olive oil
1 or 2 cloves garlic, chopped
1 large onion, sliced
2 zucchini, scrubbed and sliced (unpeeled)
1 small eggplant, peeled and cubed
3 tablespoons flour
1 red pepper, seeded and sliced
1 green pepper, seeded and sliced
3 large tomatoes, peeled, seeded and chopped
1½ tablespoons combination of fresh herbs, chopped (such as thyme,
*   oregano, summer savory) or ½ teaspoon each dried*
pinch ground coriander
salt and pepper to taste

1. In large skillet heat oil over medium heat. Add garlic and onion; sauté 5 minutes.

2. Dredge pieces of zucchini and eggplant lightly in flour and add to skillet with sliced red and green peppers. Cover and cook on low to medium heat ½ hour.

3. Add tomatoes, herbs and seasonings. Reduce heat and simmer uncovered another ½ hour. Stir occasionally. Serve either hot or cold.

Serves 5 or 6.

SOUTHERN CORN PUDDING

This can be served as an accompaniment to roast pork, beef or leg of lamb.

6 ears fresh corn
1 cup red pepper, chopped
3 eggs, beaten well
1 cup heavy cream
⅓ cup milk
1 teaspoon salt
1 teaspoon pepper
1 teaspoon granulated sugar
1½ teaspoons nutmeg

   1. Preheat oven to 350°F.
   2. Cut corn kernels from cob (approximately 2 cups). Add red pepper to corn and set aside.
   3. Mix eggs, cream, milk, salt, pepper, sugar and nutmeg.
   4. Add to corn and red pepper.
   5. Pour mixture into shallow buttered casserole dish. Place casserole in a shallow pan of warm water and bake one hour or until a knife inserted in center comes out clean.

Serves 6.

PORT O' MIAMI MARINADE

5 tablespoons fresh lemon juice, strained
½ teaspoon Creole Seasoning (see page 87)
freshly ground pepper to taste
3 tablespoons fresh parsley, chopped
3 tablespoons capers
1½ tablespoons fresh thyme or rosemary leaves, chopped
¾ cup olive oil
*¼ teaspoon toasted hot pepper sesame oil
1 cup green beans, blanched and chopped
½ cup onions, slivered
½ cup celery, chopped
2 tomatoes, chopped
lettuce leaves

   1. Whisk together lemon juice, creole seasoning, pepper, parsley, capers, herbs and oils. Add vegetables and let stand at least one hour before serving.
   2. Serve on a bed of lettuce.

Serves 4 to 6.

*Found in health or specialty food markets.

Variation: *Toss with one half pound of pasta cooked al dente.*

SPAGHETTI SQUASH CASSEROLE

3 cups spaghetti squash, cooked
2 cups sharp cheddar cheese, grated
¾ cup onions, finely chopped
¼ teaspoon nutmeg
¼ cup fine bread crumbs
½ cup Parmesan cheese, grated
1 tablespoon fresh parsley, minced
1 tablespoon butter

1. To cook squash; preheat oven to 350°F. Cut squash lengthwise and place in shallow baking dish with one inch of water. Bake 35 minutes or until tender when pierced with a fork, or microwave in five minute intervals until tender. When cool, remove seeds and scoop out squash with a fork.

2. Mix together squash, cheddar cheese, onions and nutmeg.

3. Butter a shallow baking pan, add mixture and top with bread crumbs, Parmesan cheese and parsley. Dot with butter. Recipe can be prepared in advance to this point. Just prior to serving, either bake uncovered 30 minutes in a 325°F. preheated oven, or microwave, covered with plastic wrap, in two 5-minute intervals. Broil two minutes to brown the top if using microwave oven.

Serves 4 to 6.

EGGPLANT ROLLATINE

For the sauce:
½ cup sausage (see page 128)
½ cup ground sirloin
2 cups onions, finely chopped
½ cup carrots, finely chopped
½ cup white part of leek, rinsed well, finely chopped
4 tablespoons olive oil
2 cloves garlic, minced
1 35-ounce can plum tomatoes, chopped (reserve liquid)
1 bay leaf
1 teaspoon dried thyme, crumbled
salt and pepper to taste

For the Rollatini:
2 eggplants, 1½ pound each, peeled and sliced lengthwise ¼-inch thick
¾ pound Feta cheese
1 cup ricotta cheese
1 large egg, beaten lightly
1 cup Parmesan cheese, grated
1 tablespoon fresh lemon juice
¼ cup plus 1 tablespoon fresh parsley, minced
½ cup scallions, minced
vegetable oil for brushing

1. In skillet sauté sausage and ground sirloin until pinkish brown.

2. To make sauce: In large heavy skillet cook onions, carrots and leeks in oil over moderately low heat, stirring, until vegetables are softened. Add garlic and cook mixture, stirring, 2 minutes. Add tomatoes, reserved liquid, sausage and ground sirloin, bay leaf and thyme. Bring the mixture to a boil then simmer, covered, stirring occasionally, 45 minutes. Add salt and pepper to taste and discard bay leaf. Set aside.

3. To make rollatini: Sprinkle eggplant slices lightly with salt on both sides and let drain in colander 30 minutes.

4. In food processor finely chop the Feta. Add ricotta, egg, ¾ cup Parmesan and lemon juice. Blend until smooth. Add ¼ cup parsley and scallions. Process 10 seconds.

5. Transfer eggplant slices to paper towels and pat dry. Arrange one third of the eggplant slices in one layer on jellyroll pan brushed with oil. Brush tops of eggplant with oil.

6. Cook eggplant slices under preheated broiler about 4 inches from heat, turning slices once and brushing them again with the oil, for 8 to 10 minutes, or until browned lightly on both sides. Transfer to paper towels to drain, and cook remaining slices in the same manner.

7. Preheat oven to 350°F.

8. Put 2 tablespoons of cheese mixture at short end of each eggplant slice and roll up slices to enclose filling.

9. Spread ¼ cup of the sauce in a 10 x 7 inch baking pan and arrange eggplant rolls in one layer on the sauce. Pour remaining sauce over rolls and sprinkle with remaining ¼ cup Parmesan.

10. Bake rollatini 30 to 40 minutes, or until heated through. Sprinkle with remaining 1 tablespoon parsley and serve.

Serves 4.

BROCCOLI UNDER SNOW

2 pounds broccoli florets
¾ cup mayonnaise
¼ cup sour cream
1½ teaspoons Dijon mustard
1 teaspoon Florida Key lime juice (substitute lime or lemon juice if
  you can't get Key limes)
1½ tablespoons fresh chives, minced
1½ tablespoons fresh parsley, minced
4 egg whites
pinch salt
¼ teaspoon white pepper
pinch sugar
½ cup pecans, chopped (optional)

1. Cook broccoli florets al dente and transfer to deep casserole dish.

2. Combine mayonnaise, sour cream, mustard, Key lime juice, chives and parsley in bowl and mix well.

3. Beat egg whites with salt and pepper until soft peaks form. Sprinkle with sugar and beat until stiff peaks form.

4. Fold sour cream mixture into beaten egg whites.

5. Spread mixture evenly over broccoli and pecans (if desired). Place under broiler until top is slightly browned.

Serves 6.

Variation: *Substitute green beans for brocolli and toasted, slivered almonds for pecans.*

SHERRIED YAMS WITH WALNUTS

¾ pound yams, peeled and cut into ½-inch cubes
3 tablespoons unsalted butter, cut into bits
3 tablespoons light brown sugar
1 teaspoon vanilla extract
¼ teaspoon cinnamon
3 tablespoons medium-dry Sherry
2 tablespoons walnuts, chopped and lightly toasted
salt and pepper to taste
fresh lemon juice to taste (optional)

1. In a steamer basket set over boiling water, steam the yams, covered, for 3 to 5 minutes, or until they are just tender. (Use a colander if a steamer basket is not available.)

2. In a heavy skillet combine butter, brown sugar, vanilla and cinnamon. Heat the mixture over moderate heat, stirring, until butter is melted. Stir in Sherry and cook the sauce until thickened.

3. Stir in yams, walnuts, salt and pepper to taste. Coat mixture with the sauce.

4. Sprinkle with lemon juice if desired.

Serves 2 to 3.

HARRY'S HOT LULU

One of Jackie's best friends in life, Harry Polson, was the most ardent admirer of the following dish. If he heard she was making it, he'd come to her house 2 hours early to have a shnapps and smell the heartwarming aroma.

¾ cup oil or butter
1 cup carrots, shredded
1 cup raw sweet potatoes, shredded
1 cup apple, shredded
½ cup brown sugar (or to taste)
1 cup all-purpose flour
pinch of cinnamon, nutmeg and cloves

1. Preheat oven to 350°F. Heat oil or butter in 2 quart casserole dish.

2. Mix together remaining ingredients and transfer to casserole dish.

3. Cover and bake in middle of oven for 45 minutes.

4. Uncover and bake 15 to 20 minutes more.

Serves 4.

ROASTED POTATOES WITH GARLIC

2 pounds red potatoes, peeled and cut crosswise into ¼ inch rounds
½ cup butter
4 large garlic cloves, minced
salt and pepper to taste

   1. In a heavy skillet large enough to hold potatoes in one layer, melt butter and add potatoes. Cook over moderate heat, turning occasionally, 20 minutes or until golden and tender.
   2. Add garlic, salt and pepper to taste, shaking pan occasionally, 2 minutes.

Serves 6 to 8.

SWEET POTATO BOATS

This is wonderful with turkey.

6 sweet potatoes
oil
¼ cup rum
¼ cup brandy
4 tablespoons butter
salt and freshly ground pepper to taste
½ teaspoon cinnamon
2 tablespoons brown sugar

   1. Preheat oven to 450°F. Wash sweet potatoes and rub skin with oil.
   2. Bake approximately 40 to 45 minutes, or until done.
   3. Cut each potato in half lengthwise and remove pulp. Be careful not to break the shells.
   4. Mash the pulp with rum, brandy, butter, salt and pepper.
   5. Whip mixture until smooth and fluffy and put back into shells. Sprinkle tops with cinnamon and brown sugar.
   6. Place under broiler to brown. Watch carefully to avoid burning.

Serves 12.

FIFTH STREET FRIED POTATOES

4 large red potatoes, scrubbed and sliced crosswise ⅛ inch thick
½ cup butter
salt, black pepper and cayenne to taste

1. Preheat oven to 500°F.
2. Pat potatoes dry between paper towels. Arrange in one layer in 2 buttered jelly-roll pans.
3. Generously brush potatoes with butter and bake 15 minutes, or until edges are golden brown.
4. Sprinkle with salt, black pepper and cayenne to taste.

Serves 4.

POTATOES BAKED WITH ONION-BASIL CREAM SAUCE

3 tablespoons butter
10 garlic cloves, halved
5 medium onions, sliced
2 tablespoons fresh basil, minced
salt and pepper to taste
8 to 10 medium baking potatoes, scrubbed
¼ cup plain yogurt mixed with ⅓ cup sour cream
3 tablespoons fresh parsley, minced

1. Melt butter in heavy, large skillet over medium heat. Add garlic and onions. Reduce heat to medium-low, cover and cook, stirring occasionally, about 45 minutes. Do not let brown. Blend in basil, salt and pepper and cook 3 more minutes. Cool, then place mixture in food processor or blender and purée until smooth.
2. Preheat oven to 400°F. Cut a long slit in each potato. Bake 15 minutes.
3. Reduce oven temperature to 375°F. Continue baking potatoes until soft, about 55 to 60 minutes.
4. Just before potatoes are done, blend yogurt, sour cream and parsley into the onion mixture. Place over low heat and cook until just heated through, stirring occasionally.
5. Coarsely mash potatoes in their skins and spoon sauce over tops. Serve hot.

Serves 8 to 10.

MARVELOUS MASHED POTATOES

By all means serve these with veal cutlets or roast beef like Jackie remembers having them as a child.

4 medium potatoes, peeled
½ cup skim milk, warmed
2 tablespoons butter
salt and pepper to taste
2 teaspoons fresh dill, chopped

1. Boil potatoes about 20 minutes or cut into pieces and boil about 12 minutes, or until done.
2. Drain and mash with a fork. Mix in milk, butter, salt, pepper and dill. Serve immediately.

Serves 4.

SAND POTATOES

2½ pounds red potatoes (about 9 medium)
salt
3 tablespoons oil
8 tablespoons butter
2 teaspoons garlic, minced
1 cup dry bread crumbs
Salt and freshly ground black pepper to taste

1. Preheat oven to 475°F. Scrub potatoes, put in large pot and add cold water to cover. Add 1¼ teaspoons salt per quart of water. Bring to a boil and boil slowly 15 to 20 minutes or until tender. Drain, and cut into ⅜ inch cubes.
2. Heat half the oil and half the butter in a skillet. Add half the garlic and cook until limp but not brown. Add half the potatoes and cook, tossing with a spatula, until lightly browned. Transfer to a gratin dish and keep warm, loosely covered with foil. Cook remaining potatoes in remaining oil and butter with garlic. Place into gratin dish.
3. Sprinkle bread crumbs over potatoes and season with salt and pepper to taste. Toss to coat well with crumbs. Bake on middle rack of oven for 15 minutes.
4. Put gratin dish under the broiler 4 inches from heat, for 1 minute, or until golden brown.

Serves 6.

OFRA'S PASHDIDA

When Jackie wanted something especially tasty, her dear friend Ofra would make this dish. She often served it with just a salad.

16 ounces frozen chopped spinach, cooked and drained
salt, pepper and nutmeg to taste
1 pound potatoes, peeled and thinly sliced
1 pound onions, thinly sliced
2 cups mushrooms, thinly sliced
6 ounces Gruyere or Mozzarella cheese, grated

1. Butter a 5 quart casserole dish and set aside. Preheat oven to 350°F.

2. Mix cooked spinach, salt, pepper and nutmeg.

3. Put a layer of potatoes on bottom of casserole dish. In layers, add onion, mushrooms, spinach mixture, salt, pepper and some grated cheese. Keep repeating the layers until casserole is full. Top with layer of grated cheese.

4. Bake 45 minutes.

Serves 4 as a side dish.

JACKIE'S ESCALLOPED POTATOES

This is a wonderful accompaniment to steak, roast beef, lamb chops or grilled chicken.

1 pound raw white potatoes, peeled and sliced
salt and pepper to taste
1 tablespoon fresh dill, finely chopped
¼ pound Gruyere cheese, thinly sliced
Dijon mustard (approximately 1 teaspoon)
1 pound onions, thinly sliced
½ cup dry white wine
¼ cup bread crumbs
¼ cup Parmesan cheese, grated
4 tablespoons butter

1. Preheat oven to 350°F. Thoroughly butter a 9 x 3 x 2½ inch baking pan.

2. Place one layer of potato on bottom of dish. Sprinkle with salt, pepper and a little dill. Top with layer of Gruyere cheese and spread a small amount of mustard over cheese slices. Place a layer of onion slices over cheese. Repeat procedure until dish is full. Press all the layers down well, pour wine over top layer and sprinkle with bread crumbs and Parmesan cheese.

3. Dot with butter and cover with wax paper buttered on side facing down.

4. Bake 45 minutes.

Serves 6.

Variation: *Add one layer of 1½ cups mushrooms, thinly sliced.*

MIAMI RICE

½ pound bacon strips, cut into 1-inch pieces
½ pound lean boneless pork, cut into bite-sized pieces
2 whole chicken breasts, skinned, boned and cut into bite-sized pieces
1 cup onions, chopped
3 to 4 cloves garlic, minced
1 each: red, green and yellow pepper, seeded, deribbed and cut julienne
1 14-ounce can whole tomatoes, chopped (reserve liquid)
1 tablespoon tarragon
1 tablespoon oregano
2 tablespoons Creole Seasoning (see page 87)
bay leaf
½ cup white wine
3 cups Valencia-style or Arborio rice
½ teaspoon ground saffron or saffron threads, pulverized or dissolved
    in 4 tablespoons hot broth
6 cups unsalted chicken broth or water, boiling
1 pound mussels or clams (scrubbed well)
¼ cup olive oil
4 tablespoons butter
2 pounds dolphin fillets (or other white-fleshed fish), cut into bite-sized
    pieces
4 lobster tails, body split and cut into bite-sized pieces, shells intact
16 raw shrimp, shelled and deveined with tails intact
¾ pound bay scallops (optional)
4 fresh large artichokes, steamed, leaves and chokes removed; quar-
    tered (or use a large can of artichoke hearts, drained and sliced)
½ pound snow peas
½ cup frozen sweet peas, defrosted and drained

stone crabs if in season (optional)

fresh parsley, chopped, for garnish
7 lemons, quartered, for garnish

Hot Sauce (optional)

1. In paella pan or large, shallow skillet, cook bacon then sear pork until both are browned. Over medium heat add chicken, stirring, until lightly browned. Stir in onions, garlic, pepper strips, tomatoes, reserved liquid, tarragon, oregano, 1 tablespoon Creole Seasoning and bay leaf. When mixture begins to bubble, add wine and simmer 10 minutes.

2. Preheat oven to 400°F.

3. Add rice and saffron to paella pan and stir to coat and heat rice. Over medium-high heat, add boiling broth or water, stirring until it returns to a boil and remove. Sporadically plant clams under the liquid. Cover and bake 15 minutes while cooking the seafood.

4. In separate large skillet, heat olive oil and butter over medium heat. Rinse and towel dry fish fillets and coat with remaining 1 tablespoon creole seasoning. Increase heat to medium-high, add fish and lobster pieces to skillet and sear 2 to 3 minutes. Add shrimp and scallops (if desired), and sear another 3 to 5 minutes or until shells of lobster and shrimp turn pink.

5. Remove rice mixture from oven and symetrically place seafood, artichokes, snow peas, peas and stone crabs (if desired) around paella pan. Do not stir after this point as rice will be served in this manner. Check rice for doneness and continue to bake approximately 15 minutes, or until moisture is absorbed, clams are open, ingredients are warmed and rice is tender. Garnish with lemon wedges and parsley.

6. Serve with thin Arepas (see page 24) or Cheddar Drop Biscuits (see page 178), and Hot Sauce, if desired.

Serves 10.

LAMB AND RICE PILAF

This is great for leftover leg of lamb.

1 cup cooked lamb (rare to medium rare) cut in bite-size pieces, room temperature
2 tablespoons olive oil
1 medium to large onion, chopped
½ pound mushrooms, chopped
1 cup long grain white rice
salt and pepper to taste
1 tablespoon Dijon mustard
1½ tablespoons soy sauce
1¾ cups beef broth simmered with ¼ cup red wine
2 tablespoons combination of fresh herbs, minced (such as: parsley, rosemary, thyme, tarragon, sage)
¼ cup pine nuts, toasted

1. In a skillet sauté onions and mushrooms in olive oil until soft.

2. Add rice, salt and pepper to taste. Sauté 5 minutes more.

3. Add mustard and soy sauce to simmering broth and wine. Mix, then pour into rice mixture. If there is not enough liquid to cover rice mixture add a little more wine.

4. Cover skillet with tight fitting lid and cook on low 15 minutes.

5. Add herbs and lamb, mix and cook another 5 minutes. Garnish with pine nuts before serving.

Serves 2 to 3.

PALM ISLAND PILAF

6 tablespoons butter
1 large onion, coarsely chopped
1 clove garlic, minced
½ teaspoon ground ginger
1 teaspoon ground cloves
1 teaspoon ground cardamom
1 teaspoon cinnamon
1½ cups uncooked rice, rinsed and strained
⅛ teaspoon saffron (or a pinch)
¾ cup fresh mint leaves, finely chopped
½ cup fresh cilantro, finely chopped
1 large tomato, sliced
¾ cup fresh green peas
3 carrots, finely chopped
1 cup raisins
3 cups chicken broth
½ teaspoon salt
1 cup pine nuts, toasted

1. In large skillet heat butter and sauté onion until soft.

2. Stir in garlic, ginger, cloves, cardamom, cinnamon and rice. Sauté several minutes.

3. Add saffron, mint, cilantro, tomato slices, peas, carrots, and raisins. Stir well.

4. Add chicken broth and salt.

5. Bring to a boil, reduce heat to low, cover and cook 20 minutes.

6. Transfer to serving platter and garnish with pine nuts.

Serves 4.

RISOTTO "BERMUDA STYLE"

3 tablespoons butter
1 large Bermuda onion, peeled and chopped
1½ cups Arborio rice
½ cup dry Marsala wine
*¼ cup porcini mushrooms, chopped
¼ teaspoon saffron
pinch nutmeg
4½ to 5 cups chicken broth, boiling
½ cup Parmesan cheese, freshly grated
salt and pepper to taste

1. Melt butter, add onion and sauté a few minutes.

2. Add rice. Use a wooden spoon and stir about one minute over medium heat.

3. With wooden spoon stir in wine until absorbed.

4. Add mushrooms and stir.

5. Add saffron and nutmeg. Add simmering broth, about ¼ to ½ cup at a time, stirring constantly. As rice absorbs the broth, continue adding all but ¼ cup of the liquid. This process should take approximately 18 to 20 minutes.

6. When rice is cooked, add reserved ¼ cup broth and remove from heat.

7. Immediately add Parmesan cheese, salt and pepper and stir vigorously. Serve immediately.

Serves 4.

*Use fresh if available, otherwise use canned. If dried, soak 20 minutes before using.

RICE MEXICANA

2 cups Spanish, extra long-grain rice
hot water
2 onions, chopped
3 cloves garlic, chopped
3 cups chicken broth
¼ cup vegetable oil
1½ cups tomatoes, peeled, seeded and pureed in blender or
    food processor (see page 95)
salt and pepper to taste
½ cup peas, cooked

For garnish:
6 jalepeño peppers (hot) or 6 Mexican chilies (mild)
1 avocado, peeled, pitted and sliced
fresh parsley sprigs

1. In a bowl let rice soak 20 minutes in hot water to cover. Drain in large sieve, rinse under cold water then drain in sieve 30 minutes.

2. In blender or food processor purée onions and garlic, adding 1 to 2 tablespoons broth if necessary.

3. In a pan sauté rice in oil with onion mixture over moderate heat, stirring occasionally, 5 minutes. Stir in tomato and cook, stirring 2 minutes. Add remaining broth and salt and pepper to taste. Bring liquid to a boil, cover and cook rice over low heat 18 to 20 minutes, or until liquid is absorbed.

4. Stir in peas and cook mixture, tossing with a fork, until peas are heated through.

5. Serve rice garnished with hot peppers, avocado, and parsley.

Serves 6.

WILD RICE WITH PECANS, PISTACHIOS AND APPLES

1½ cups wild rice
5 cups chicken broth
⅓ cup olive oil
1 cup onions, chopped
1 cup sausage
1 cup chicken livers (boiled 5 minutes and chopped)
1 cup pecans
½ cup Granny Smith apples, chopped
½ cup golden raisins
½ cup dark raisins
½ cup pistachios
4 scallions, thinly sliced
⅓ cup orange juice
1 teaspoon salt
1 teaspoon black pepper

1. Put rice in strainer and rinse thoroughly under cold water.
2. Place rice in medium-size heavy saucepan. Add broth and bring to a boil; reduce heat and simmer 45 minutes. Drain in colander and place in bowl.
3. Meanwhile, sauté onions in olive oil until golden. Add sausage; sauté until brown and add chicken livers.
4. Combine chicken liver mixture with rice and all other ingredients. Let stand 1½ hours.
5. Preheat oven to 325°F. Bake 30 minutes and serve warm.

Serves 6 to 8.

SPICY DIRTY RICE

2 to 2½ cups hot, cooked rice

Rice Dressing:

3 tablespoons vegetable oil
2 tablespoons all-purpose flour
¾ pound lean boneless pork, minced
½ pound sausage meat
3 medium onions, chopped
2 stalks celery, chopped
1 small green pepper, seeded and chopped
1 small red pepper, seeded and chopped
3 cloves garlic, minced
1 pound chicken livers
3 scallions with tops, chopped
1 tablespoon butter
1 10-ounce can condensed chicken broth (or 10 ounces homemade chicken broth)
½ cup hot water
2 teaspoons Creole Seasoning (or to taste) recipe follows
1 teaspoon red hot pepper sauce
3 tablespoons fresh parsley sprigs as garnish

1. Cook 2 tablespoons vegetable oil and flour in small heavy saucepan over low heat, stirring frequently, until roux is the color of dark mahogany, about 45 minutes (roux must be cooked until very dark but not burned; do not undercook).

2. While roux is cooking, sauté pork and sausage meat in remaining 1 tablespoon oil in Dutch oven or heavy pot until brown, about 10 minutes. Add onions, celery, green and red peppers and garlic. Cook, stirring and scraping bottom of pan, for 20 minutes.

3. Sauté livers and scallions in butter in a small saucepan until livers are no longer pink inside, about 5 minutes, and finely chop.

4. Stir liver mixture, chicken broth, water, Creole Seasoning, red pepper sauce and roux into pork and sausage mixture; reduce heat. Simmer covered over low heat 45 minutes; simmer uncovered 20 minutes.

5. Stir in as much rice as needed to make a moist dressing. Garnish with parsley.

Serves 4.

CREOLE SEASONING

Keep a batch of this with other seasoning staples and use when a spicier flavor than simply salt is desired.

⅓ cup plus 1 tablespoon salt
⅓ cup plus 1 tablespoon paprika
⅓ cup cayenne pepper
¼ cup black pepper
¼ cup granulated garlic powder
1 tablespoon onion powder
3 tablespoons thyme

1. Combine all ingredients and store in an airtight container.

Makes nearly 2 cups.

MORROCCAN RICE

1½ teaspoons cumin
1 cup hot water
8 ounces Feta cheese
¼ cup clarified butter (see page 155)
¼ cup vegetable oil
½ cup pistachio nuts
2 onions, chopped
2 tablespoons garlic, minced
3 tablespoons fresh ginger root, minced
2 teaspoons curry powder
1 teaspoon cinnamon
1 teaspoon allspice
up to 1 teaspoon cayenne pepper to taste
1 teaspoon black pepper
1 cup green peas
1 cup broccoli florets
2 cups long-grain white rice
2 teaspoons salt
4 cups boiling water
½ cup dark raisins
½ cup golden raisins
fresh parsley, chopped, for garnish

1. Mix cumin with 1 cup hot water. Add cheese, mix and set aside.
2. Place butter and oil in large skillet over medium-high heat. Sauté pistachio nuts until browned, 2 to 3 minutes, and remove with a slotted spoon. Set aside.
3. Add onion, garlic, ginger, curry powder, cinnamon, allspice, cayenne and black pepper to pan. Sauté until onions are golden, about 5 minutes. Add peas and broccoli and sauté 2 minutes longer.
4. Into the same pan add rice, salt and boiling water. Cover, bring to a fresh boil; lower heat, simmer 20 to 25 minutes to absorb all liquids. Remove from heat.
5. Stir in cheese mixture, pistachio nuts and raisins.
6. Place in serving dish, sprinkle with parsley and serve.

Serves 10 to 12.

SESAME BASMATI RICE

*1 cup basmati rice, rinsed well
*1 tablespoon toasted sesame oil
 1 tablespoon olive oil
 2 cloves garlic, crushed
 1¾ cups water, boiling
 ¼ teaspoon salt, or to taste
 pepper to taste
 1 tablespoon sesame seeds, toasted
 soy sauce (optional)

1. In a 2 quart saucepan, heat the oils over medium high heat; add rice and garlic and stir approximately 5 minutes to coat the grains.

2. Add water, salt and pepper to taste and bring to a boil. Reduce heat, cover and simmer 15 to 20 minutes, or until liquid is absorbed and rice is tender but not soggy.

3. Just before serving, gently toss in sesame seeds.

4. Guests may add soy sauce as desired.

Serves 4.

*Found in specialty supermarkets or health food stores.

WILD RICE CASSEROLE

This dish may be prepared a day in advance and baked just prior to serving. Double the recipe and freeze half for future use.

1 cup wild rice, rinsed and drained
6 cups boiling water
½ teaspoon salt
1 tablespoon butter
1 cup onions, chopped
¼ cup celery, chopped
1 cup sharp cheddar cheese, grated
1 28-ounce can whole tomatoes, undrained and chopped
1 cup frozen peas, defrosted and drained
1 teaspoon oregano
2 tablespoons Parmesan cheese

1. Stir rice into 3 cups boiling water and let boil, uncovered, 5 minutes. Remove from heat, cover and let set at least one hour. Rinse and drain.
2. Bring remaining 3 cups water to a boil; add salt and rice. Reduce heat, cover and simmer 30 minutes. Drain and transfer to large mixing bowl.
3. Preheat oven to 350°F. and butter a 2 quart casserole dish.
4. Sauté onions and celery in butter and add to rice. Add remaining ingredients, except Parmesan cheese, and mix well. Transfer to casserole dish, top with Parmesan cheese and bake 45 minutes.

Serves 6.

SPICY SPINACH RICE CASSEROLE WITH MUSHROOMS

4 tablespoons butter
2 cloves garlic, crushed
4 tablespoons shallots, chopped, or 2 tablespoons dried shallots
2 cups mushrooms, sliced
2½ cups wild rice blend
4 cups chicken broth, boiling
10 ounces frozen chopped spinach, defrosted and drained
1 cup Parmesan cheese, grated
¼ teaspoon cayenne pepper

1. Preheat oven to 350°F and butter a 2 quart casserole dish.
2. In skillet over medium heat, melt butter; add garlic, shallots, mushrooms and rice blend. Stir to coat the grains.
3. Add broth to rice and stir lightly. Add remaining ingredients, toss and transfer to casserole dish. Bake 35 minutes.

Serves 8.

CLARIBEL'S WILD RICE WITH MUSHROOMS AND ALMONDS

¼ cup plus 1 tablespoon butter
½ cup almonds, slivered
2 tablespoons scallions or chives, chopped
2 tablespoons green pepper, chopped
1 pound Shitake mushrooms, chopped
1 cup wild rice, rinsed and drained
3 cups chicken broth
2 tablespoons cognac
1 tablespoon soy sauce
pepper to taste
2 stalks celery, finely chopped
2 cloves garlic, minced

1. Preheat oven to 400°F.

2. Melt butter in pot or saucepan and sauté almonds until lightly browned. Add scallions, green pepper, mushrooms and rice. Sauté about 15 minutes, stirring often.

3. Stir in chicken broth and cognac. Cover and simmer 30 minutes.

4. Pour into buttered baking dish and bake, covered, 45 minutes and uncovered 5 minutes.

5. Sauté celery in remaining 1 tablespoon butter approximately 1 minute and stir into rice mixture while celery is still crisp. Serve with almonds sprinkled on top. Season with soy sauce and pepper before serving.

Serves 4.

BEACH BERRY RICE

1 cup short grain brown rice
*¹⁄₃ cup wheat berries
2 tablespoons butter
1 tablespoon olive oil
1 clove garlic, crushed
2 cups water, boiling
¹⁄₂ cup pine nuts
*2 teaspoons Tamari sauce
¹⁄₄ cup combination of fresh herbs, chopped (such as basil, cilantro, oregano, thyme)

1. Wash grains well and drain.

2. In a 2 quart saucepan, heat 1 tablespoon butter and the oil; add rice, wheat berries and garlic. Stir approximately 5 minutes to coat the grains.

3. Add boiling water, pine nuts and Tamari sauce. Bring to full boil, reduce heat, cover and simmer 45 minutes, or until liquid evaporates.

4. Just before serving, stir in remaining 1 tablespoon butter and herbs (if desired).

Serves 6.

*Found in health food stores.

HERBED RISOTTO WITH ASPARAGUS

This is a great Sunday lunch with a salad.

1½ pounds fresh asparagus
2 tablespoons olive oil
1 medium onion, finely minced
salt and pepper to taste
1½ cups Arborio rice
½ cup dry white wine
4½ to 5 cups chicken broth, boiling
1 cup Parmesan cheese, grated
½ tablespoon butter
1 cup combination of fresh herbs, finely chopped (such as chives, basil, parsley, thyme and tarragon)

1. Wash asparagus and cut into small pieces, about ½ inch long – use only top half of asparagus.

2. In skillet heat oil and sauté onion 2 minutes. Add asparagus pieces and salt and pepper; sauté one more minute. Add rice and stir about one minute.

3. With wooden spoon stir in wine until absorbed.

4. Set on medium heat. Add simmering chicken broth, ¼ to ½ cup at a time, stirring constantly. As rice absorbs the broth, add more until all but ¼ cup has been used. This process should take about 18 to 20 minutes.

5. When rice is cooked, add ¼ cup reserved broth and remove from heat immediately.

6. Stir in Parmesan cheese, butter and herbs.

Serves 4.

LINGUINE WITH AVOCADO & ROSEMARY

2 ripe tomatoes, seeded and chopped
2 tablespoons olive oil
½ cup butter
3 to 4 large garlic cloves, peeled and crushed
4 large sprigs fresh rosemary, leaves removed from stems
1 beef boullion cube, crushed
1 pound linguine
½ large, ripe but firm avocado, peeled and cut into bite-sized pieces
½ pound fresh Mozzarella cheese, cut into bite-sized pieces
⅓ cup Parmesan cheese, freshly grated
freshly ground pepper

   1. Sauté tomatoes in olive oil 5 minutes and set aside.
   2. At same time melt butter in separate pan. Add garlic and whole rosemary leaves and cook 5 minutes, or until rosemary and garlic are crisp. Add crushed boullion cube and cook until dissolved. Set mixture aside.
   3. Cook linguine al dente. Drain and toss with tomatoes, rosemary sauce, avocado and Mozzarella. Serve with Parmesan cheese and freshly ground pepper.

Serves 4.

LINGUINE WITH WALNUT CREAM SAUCE

1½ cups walnuts
¾ cup half and half (half milk, half cream)
½ cup packed fresh parsley sprigs
4 tablespoons olive oil
2 large garlic cloves, minced
8 fresh basil leaves
pinch cayenne pepper
salt to taste
¾ pound linguine

   1. Pulse in food processor walnuts, half and half, parsley, oil, garlic, basil, cayenne and salt to taste until mixture is blended but not smooth.
   2. Cook linguine al dente and drain. Place in heated serving bowl and toss with sauce.

Serves 4 to 6.

LOBSTER AND LINGUINE IN BASIL TOMATO SAUCE

*2 cups fresh tomatoes, peeled, seeded and coarsely chopped
(substitute canned, whole tomatoes, puréed)*
⅓ cup olive oil
4 to 6 cloves garlic, finely sliced
1 tablespoon hot chili pepper, minced
½ teaspoon salt
¼ teaspoon freshly ground pepper
1 pound lobster meat, de-shelled, cubed and uncooked
*2 lobster tails (approximaely 1 pound each), thawed if frozen; meat
removed and cut into ¾ inch cubes*
1½ cups fresh basil leaves, coarsely chopped
1 pound fresh linguine, vermicelli, or other thin, preferably fresh noodles
½ cup Feta cheese, crumbled

1. To prepare tomatoes; drop in large pot of boiling water and remove
when skins begin to crack – approximately 30 to 60 seconds. Let cool
and peel. Cut out stem, slice in half crosswise and gently squeeze seeds
and juice into a bowl. Strain, discard seeds and reserve juice. Chop
tomatoes. Set aside.

2. In large skillet, heat oil over medium heat, add garlic slices and
minced chili pepper. As soon as garlic begins to bubble around the
edges, add tomatoes, reserved tomato liquid, salt and pepper. Reduce
heat and simmer 10 minutes.

3. In the meantime, boil enough water to cover pasta.

4. Increase heat on sauce to medium; when it begins to bubble add
lobster, then basil. Add pasta to boiling water.

5. For best results, cook lobster and pasta simultaneously. Constantly
stir lobster. Remove from heat as soon as it turns white, approximately
3 to 5 minutes. Remove pasta when it is al dente.

6. Drain pasta, transfer to a serving platter, pour lobster and sauce
over linguine. Top with Feta cheese crumbs. Serve immediately.

Serves 6.

Note: *Shrimp may be substituted for or used in addition to lobster.*

ANGEL HAIR PASTA WITH MACADAMIA NUT PESTO

3 cups fresh basil leaves
3 cloves garlic
1 cup macadamia nuts
½ teaspoon salt
½ teaspoon freshly ground pepper
¾ cup olive oil
½ cup Parmesan cheese, grated
3 tablespoons Romano cheese, grated
½ pound fresh angel hair pasta
3 tablespoons unsalted butter, room temperature (optional)
8 whole basil leaves, for garnish
1 tomato, chopped, for garnish

1. In blender or food processor, process basil, garlic, ½ cup of the nuts, salt, pepper and ¼ cup olive oil until consistency is smooth.

2. Slowly add remaining ½ cup olive oil while processing. Stir in cheeses and set aside.

3. Preheat oven to 250°F. Coarsely chop remaining ½ cup macadamia nuts, place one layer deep on baking sheet and bake 10 minutes to lightly toast. Turn frequently.

4. Cook pasta al dente, drain, and toss with sauce and butter (if desired). Transfer to serving dish, top with toasted nuts and garnishes. Serve immediately.

Serves 4.

ANGEL HAIR PASTA WITH BROCOLLI PESTO AND RED PEPPER

1 pound angel hair pasta
2 cups broccoli florets
½ cup fresh basil leaves, coarsely chopped
¼ cup garlic chives, finely chopped
¼ cup pine nuts (pecans or walnuts may be substituted)
½ teaspoon salt
¼ teaspoon fresh pepper
1 cup olive oil
1 large clove garlic
½ cup Parmesan cheese, finely grated
¾ cup sweet red pepper, chopped

   1. Cook pasta al dente, drain and cool to room temperature.
   2. In blender or food processor, purée broccoli, basil, chives, nuts, salt, pepper, oil and garlic until smooth. Stir in cheese.
   3. Toss broccoli pesto, pasta and ½ cup of the red pepper together. Transfer to serving dish, top with remaining red pepper and serve.

Serves 4.

SPICY SZECHUAN NOODLES

½ cup plus 2 tablespoons chunky peanut butter
5 tablespoons peanut oil
5 tablespoons scallions, minced
3 tablespoons soy sauce
2 tablespoons rice wine vinegar
3 teaspoons garlic, crushed
1 teaspoon sugar
*2 tablespoons Hoisin sauce
*½ teaspoon oriental Hot Oil
1 pound Chinese egg noodles
3 scallions, cut in ½ inch pieces, for garnish

1. Combine peanut butter, oil, scallions, soy sauce, vinegar, garlic, sugar, Hoisin sauce and Hot Oil in small bowl. Blend well. Add water if thinner consistency is desired for sauce.

2. Cook noodles al dente, drain and transfer to serving bowl.

3. Add sauce; toss lightly. Garnish with scallion pieces.

Serves 8 to 10.

*Available at Chinese grocery stores.

FETTUCINE WITH SMOKED SALMON

4 cups heavy whipping cream
⅔ cup butter
1 pound nova (smoked salmon), cut julienne
¼ cup chives, minced
¼ cup basil, minced
1 teaspoon garlic, minced
freshly ground pepper
1 pound fettucine
parsley sprigs for garnish

1. Combine cream and butter in medium saucepan. Cook on medium-high heat until thick, glossy and reduced by half.

2. Add salmon, chives, basil, garlic and pepper. Cook, stirring gently, about 1 minute. Transfer to serving platter.

3. Cook fettucine al dente, drain and lightly toss together with remaining ingredients. Garnish with parsley and serve.

Serves 6.

THIN SPAGHETTI WITH CLAM SAUCE

5 mushrooms, chopped
1 medium onion, chopped
1 tablespoon olive oil
2 cans (6½ ounces each) minced clams
1½ cups liquid (combination of clam juice, ⅓ cup dry white wine
*   and chicken broth)*
2 tablespoons butter
2 tablespoons flour
2 tablespoons combination of fresh herbs, chopped (such as parsley,
*   tarragon, chives, thyme, oregano, basil)*
salt and pepper to taste
1 pound thin spaghetti

1. Sauté mushrooms and onions in olive oil and set aside.
2. Drain clams. Combine juice, wine and chicken broth to make 1½ cups liquid. Add bottled clam juice and use less chicken broth if desired .
3. Melt butter in skillet, add flour and whisk until smooth. Add liquid and cook on medium heat until thickened.
4. Add clams, mushrooms, onions, herbs, salt and pepper to taste. Cook on low to medium heat 5 minutes.
5. Just before serving cook spaghetti al dente, drain and toss with sauce. Serve hot.

Serves 4.

41ST STREET NOODLE KUGEL

This should warm the hearts of all who eat it. It's good for lunch and good for you.

12 ounces broad egg noodles
4 tablespoons butter, room temperature
4 eggs, beaten well
6 tablespoons granulated sugar
20 ounces sour cream
1 teaspoon salt
12 ounces dry-curd cottage cheese
2/3 cup milk
2 teaspoons vanilla extract

Topping:
4 tablespoons brown sugar
2 teaspoons cinnamon
4 tablespoons butter, melted
3/4 cup cornflakes, finely crushed

1. Cook and drain noodles. Add butter and stir until melted.

2. In separate bowl beat eggs and sugar. Add sour cream and salt and mix well.

3. Blend in cottage cheese, milk and vanilla. Stir in noodles.

4. Preheat oven to 350°F. and butter a pyrex casserole dish. Transfer noodles to dish and bake 25 minutes.

5. Combine topping ingredients, spread over kugel and bake another 20 minutes.

Serves 8.

JOAN'S 4TH OF JULY FETTUCINE

¾ cup pine nuts
½ cup butter, or more to taste
1 large onion, chopped
8 large cloves garlic, minced
8 fresh medium shitake mushrooms, stems removed and sliced (if necessary, substitute dried, soaked in hot water 15 minutes before using)
¼ cup green olives, chopped
*⅓ cup sun-dried tomatoes (packed in oil), sliced into thin strips
2 large ripe tomatoes, coarsely chopped
½ cup frozen peas, thawed
¾ pound spinach fettucine
½ cup Feta cheese or to taste, crumbled, as garnish
¼ cup fresh basil, chopped, as garnish

1. Melt butter in large skillet over medium heat, add pine nuts and sauté 7 to 10 minutes until golden. Remove.

2. Add onion and garlic and sauté until soft. Add mushrooms, sun-dried tomatoes and olives. Sauté 10 minutes over low to medium heat, stirring periodically.

3. Add tomatoes and peas and cook 10 minutes or until tomatoes are soft. At this point add more butter if desired.

4. Cook pasta al dente, drain and toss with sauce and pine nuts. Transfer to serving dish, top with Feta cheese and basil. Serve immediately.

Serves 4.

*Found in specialty food markets.

LASAGNA WITH MEATBALLS

Meatball Ingredients:
1 pound lean ground beef
½ pound ground veal
¼ pound ground pork
1 egg
3 tablespoons onion, chopped
3 tablespoons Parmesan cheese, grated
1 clove garlic, minced
2 tablespoons parsley flakes
1 teaspoon oregano
¾ teaspoon salt
¼ teaspoon pepper

Sauce Ingredients:
¼ cup olive oil
1 clove garlic, minced
1 small onion, chopped
1 large can (1 pound, 12 ounces) whole tomatoes, coarsely
    chopped (reserve liquid)
1 12-ounce can tomato paste
2 teaspoons oregano
1 teaspoon basil
1 teaspoon sugar
1 teaspoon salt
½ teaspoon savory
¼ teaspoon pepper
¾ cup water

Other Ingredients:
*2 to 3 sheets fresh spinach lasagna pasta
1 pound Mozzarella cheese, grated
1 pound ricotta cheese
1½ cups Parmesan cheese, grated

1. Thoroughly combine all meatball ingredients in mixing bowl. Shape into small balls ½ inch round and set aside.

2. In large, heavy saucepot, heat oil and lightly brown meatballs; then remove, reserving oil.

3. To make sauce, sauté garlic and onions in reserved oil. Add remaining sauce ingredients, stirring over medium heat, until mixture boils. Reduce heat and simmer two hours, stirring occasionally.

4. Preheat oven to 350°F. Cook lasagna noodles al dente; drain and cut to fit baking dish as needed.

5. In large baking dish sprinkle a little sauce on the bottom. Layer one-half of each of the ingredients: first noodles, then Mozzarella, ricotta, meatballs, tomato sauce and Parmesan cheese. Repeat layers with remainder of each of the ingredients.

6. Bake 45 minutes. If freezing, let defrost before baking.

Serves 8.

If fresh pasta is not available, substitute ½ pound packaged lasagna noodles and cook as directed on package.

PASTA PARMESANO

8 ounces imported Parmesan cheese, room temperature
1 pound fettucine
2 teaspoons salt
⅔ cup unsalted butter, cut into 8 pieces, room temperature
1 teaspoon fresh garlic, minced
2 cups whipping cream, room temperature
½ teaspoon nutmeg

1. Grate Parmesan cheese on hand grater.
2. Cook pasta al dente and drain well.
3. Transfer pasta to large bowl. Add butter and garlic; toss lightly. Blend in cheese and cream. Add nutmeg and toss. Serve immediately.

Serves 4.

Seafood

SEAFOOD SOUFFLÉ

6 ounces lobster meat, cooked and coarsely chopped
4 ounces shrimp, cooked and coarsely chopped
4 tablespoons butter
5 tablespoons flour
1½ cups milk
6 eggs, separated
1 teaspoon Creole Seasoning (see page 87)
¼ cup dry white wine
1 tablespoon fresh thyme, chopped
½ teaspoon white pepper
2 pinches cream of tartar
melted butter for greasing

1. Prepare seafood and set aside.

2. In small saucepan, melt butter over medium-low heat, whisk in flour and cook until golden in color. Slowly whisk in milk. When mixture begins to simmer, transfer to large, stainless steel mixing bowl.

3. Add egg yolks, wine, seafood and all seasonings except cream of tartar. Mix well.

4. Preheat oven to 350°F. Grease sides and bottom of a two quart soufflé container (either one large or six small) with melted butter.

5. Using a stainless steel, copper or glass bowl, beat egg whites to a stiff peak. Add cream of tartar near end of process.

6. Fold egg whites into seafood mixture with a large, rubber spatula. Be careful not to overmix.

7. Pour into soufflé dish(es) up to ¾ full and bake 25 minutes. Increase heat to 375°F. and bake 20 minutes more.

Serves 4 to 6.

SHRIMP CREOLE

1½ pounds shrimp
4 tablespoons plus 1 teaspoon butter
2 cups onion, chopped
1½ cups celery, chopped
1 green pepper, seeded and cut into 1 inch pieces
1 clove garlic, minced
3 cups ripe tomatoes, peeled and cut into 1 inch pieces.
3 tablespoons fresh basil, chopped
2 teaspoons thyme, chopped
1 bay leaf
Tabasco sauce (a few drops)
1 teaspoon grated lemon rind
salt and pepper to taste
1 teaspoon flour
3 tablespoons parsley, chopped
juice of ½ a lemon
2 tablespoons Pernod

1. Clean and devein shrimp. Set aside.
2. Melt 4 tablespoons butter in large skillet. Add onion and cook until translucent. Add celery, green pepper and garlic. Cook 3 minutes.
3. Add tomatoes, basil, thyme, bay leaf, Tabasco, lemon rind, salt and pepper. Cook uncovered 15 minutes.
4. Add shrimp. Cook 3 minutes more.
5. Mix together 1 teaspoon butter and 1 teaspoon flour. Add mixture, little by little, to simmering sauce, stirring constantly. Cook 1 minute; add parsley, lemon juice and Pernod.

Serves 4.

HOT PEPPER SHRIMP

A pungent dish, heady with garlic and hot pepper. Serve with Spicy Dirty Rice.

1 cup peanut or vegetable oil
juice of 5 limes
5 cloves garlic, minced
3 tablespoons parsley, minced
½ teaspoon hot red pepper flakes
2 pounds large shrimp (about 36), shelled (tails left intact), deveined
½ teaspoon salt

1. Combine oil, lime juice, garlic, parsley and pepper flakes in small bowl. Mix well. Pour over shrimp in medium bowl; toss to coat. Refrigerate, covered, overnight.

2. Preheat broiler. Remove shrimp from marinade; arrange in single layer on broiler pan. Sprinkle evenly with salt. Broil 3 to 4 inches from heat until shrimp begin to turn white, about 1½ minutes. Turn shrimp over and cook until firm, about 2 minutes.

3. Serve over Spicy Dirty Rice (see page 86).

Serves 6.

GERHARD'S SPICY SHRIMP ON FRIED GREEN PLANTAINS

½ cup of fresh orange juice
½ cup of pineapple juice
1 orange – grated zest only
½ teaspoon of cumin powder
2 cinnamon sticks
½ teaspoon cayenne pepper
1 teaspoon tabasco
1 teaspoon salt
1 tablespoon sesame oil
16 jumbo shrimp (approximately 1½ pounds)
2 peeled green plantains cut crosswise in ½ inch slices
½ cup peanut oil for frying
1 tablespoon of chopped parsley

1. Combine all ingredients except shrimp, plantains and parsley in a saucepan, bring to a boil and cook for 2 minutes.

2. Place shrimp in a glass or ceramic bowl and pour boiling marinade over them. Allow to cool to room temperature – cover and refrigerate overnight.

3. In a 12″ skillet, heat the oil over medium heat. Add as many plantain slices at one time without crowding the pan and brown them for about 2 minutes on each side. Remove and let the plantains drain on a paper towel. On a board using a solid spatula, press each slice into a flat round about ½ inch thick and 1½ inches in diameter. Reheat the oil and fry the plantains for about 1 minute on each side and drain on a paper towel.

4. Center plantains on a plater and arrange the shrimp around them. Spoon the marinade over the shrimp and sprinkle with chopped parsley. Shrimp can be served cold or at room temperature.

Serves 4.

SHRIMP WITH SHERRY CREAM SAUCE

1½ cups butter
6 garlic cloves, minced
36 large shrimp, shelled and deveined
4 cups mushrooms, sliced
3 cups heavy cream
12 tablespoons sweet Sherry or Red Port
1½ teaspoons dried basil
1 pound linguine, cooked al dente
4 tablespoons brandy

1. Melt butter in large skillet over medium heat. Add garlic and sauté briefly, about 2 to 3 minutes; do not brown. Add shrimp and sauté until they just begin to turn pink.

2. Remove shrimp. Add mushrooms, increase heat and sauté briefly. Remove with slotted spoon.

3. Add cream, Sherry and basil and simmer until sauce is reduced and slightly thickened.

4. Return shrimp and mushrooms to skillet and heat sauce through.

5. Prepare linguine; drain, set aside and keep warm.

6. Warm brandy in small saucepan until barely lukewarm, pour over sauce and ignite.

7. Pour shrimp and sauce over prepared linguine. Serve immediately.

Serves 6 to 8.

ORIENTAL BRAISED LOBSTER

2 large egg whites
2 tablespoons cornstarch
3 cups plus 2 tablespoons vegetable oil
salt and pepper to taste
2 one pound lobster tails, thawed if frozen, meat removed and
    cut into ¾ inch cubes
1 small onion, minced
4 teaspoons ginger root, peeled and minced
4 garlic cloves, minced
*¾ cup Hoisin sauce
4 tablespoons dry Sherry
1 tablespoon sugar
3 teaspoons soy sauce
*2 teaspoons Chinese chili paste
*1 teaspoon Oriental sesame oil
¾ cup scallions, chopped

1. In a small bowl combine egg whites, cornstarch, 2 tablespoons vegetable oil, and salt and pepper to taste. Stir in lobster and marinate 10 minutes.

2. In a wok heat remaining 3 cups vegetable oil to 300°F., or until a haze appears. Cook lobster in oil, stirring 45 seconds to 1 minute, or until cooked through. Transfer lobster with a slotted spoon to paper towels to drain, keeping it warm. Pour off all but 5 tablespoons of oil from the wok.

3. In remaining oil cook onion, ginger root and garlic over high heat, stirring 30 seconds. Return lobster to wok. Add Hoisin sauce, Sherry, sugar, soy sauce and chili paste. Cook mixture 45 seconds to 1 minute, or until sauce is thickened slightly.

4. Transfer lobster mixture to heated platter. Drizzle with sesame oil and sprinkle with scallions.

Serves 4 or 6.

*Found in specialty food markets.

CRISPY DOLPHIN FINGERS

Everybody's favorite fish! Double the breading recipe and store in refrigerator for later use.

Breading:
1 cup unbleached all-purpose flour
1 cup dry bread crumbs
1 tablespoon dill
1 tablespoon thyme
1 teaspoon orange peel, grated
1 teaspoon savory
1 teaspoon oregano
3 tablespoons dried onion flakes (instant, minced onion)
1 teaspoon salt
½ teaspoon black pepper

Other Ingredients:
2 eggs, lightly beaten
3 tablespoons olive oil, or more as needed
3 tablespoons butter
2 to 3 pounds fresh dolphin fillets, bones and blood line removed;
    cut into 1 inch x 3 inch finger portions
lemon or lime wedges
watercress and tomato tomato wedges as garnish
1 recipe Fisherman's Sauce (to follow)
1 recipe Alex's Alioli Sauce (to follow)

1. To make breading, mix all dry ingredients together and set aside.

2. Lightly beat eggs in a bowl and add fish. Cover and refrigerate up to several hours if desired.

3. Just prior to serving, heat butter and oil in a large skillet over medium-high heat. With one hand remove fish from eggs, one at a time, and with the other hand (to prevent batter-coated fingers) coat fish well in breading mixture. Line breaded fish on wax paper.

4. Add only enough fish to hot oil and butter to avoid crowding the pan; sauté three minutes on each side, or until browned. Drain on paper towels. Fast and furious is the key to a crispy outside and tender inside. If more oil is needed allow it to become hot enough before adding more fish. This will ensure crispness.

5. Transfer to serving dish, garnish with lime or lemon wedges, watercress and tomato wedges.

6. Serve with either Fisherman's Sauce or Alex's Alioli Sauce.

Serves 4 to 6.

FISHERMAN'S SAUCE

This is a type of tartar sauce and may be prepared several days in advance.

1 cup mayonnaise
⅓ cup sweet pickle relish, drained
1½ tablespoons fresh lime juice
1 tablespoon capers, drained and minced
1 teaspoon parsley flakes
1 teaspoon oregano flakes
1 tablespoon onion, finely grated or minced
⅛ teaspoon salt
dash pepper

1. Whisk all ingredients together in small serving bowl.
2. Cover and refrigerate 1 to 2 hours before using.

Makes 1⅓ cups.

ALEX'S ALIOLI SAUCE

This sauce is a special recipe from Alex which was served at his "Tapas Bar and Grill" in the Betsy Ross Hotel in South Miami Beach. It's also sensational as a dipping sauce for meats, potatoes, or let your imagination be your guide. Unfortunately, the restaurant is gone – but the sauce remains!

1 egg plus 1 egg yolk
¼ teaspoon Dijon mustard
1 teaspoon salt
2 tablespoons fresh lemon juice
1 cup olive oil
4 to 5 cloves garlic, mashed to a paste

1. In bowl of blender or food processor place whole egg, egg yolk, mustard, salt and lemon juice. Blend a few seconds.
2. With the motor running, gradually pour in oil and continue blending until thickened and silky.
3. Add garlic, blend well and "good appetite" from Alex.

Makes 1½ cups.

BROILED SOFT-SHELLED CRABS

12 soft-shelled crabs (ready to cook)
flour for dredging
3 tablespoons olive oil or vegetable oil
½ cup parsley, chopped
1 tablespoon chives, chopped
2 teaspoons paprika
1 teaspoon salt
fresh lemon juice
lemon wedges as garnish

1. Preheat broiler.
2. Dredge crabs lightly with flour. Arrange on broiling rack.
3. Mix oil with parsley, chives, paprika and salt. Brush mixture on crabs.
4. Broil crabs 5 to 8 minutes. Baste often and turn once during cooking. Serve with lemon juice in dipping bowls. Garnish with lemon wedges.

Serves 4.

MUSSELS MARINIÉRE

2½ pounds mussels
3 tablespoons butter
1 medium size onion, chopped
3 sprigs parsley, chopped (3 tablespoons)
fresh ground pepper to taste
¾ cup dry white wine

1. Clean mussels under cold water and drain.
2. In a pot big enough to hold mussels, heat butter and cook onions. Add mussels, half the parsley, the pepper and wine. Cover and cook 5 minutes or until mussels open.
3. Place mussels in 4 separate serving bowls and distribute liquid over mussels. Garnish with remaining parsley.

Serves 4.

COMMON SENSE ISN'T"
ANON.

"ROBBING A BANK IS NO CRIME - COMPARED TO OWNING ONE"
BERTOLDT BRECHT

"ANYONE WHO WISHES TO RETAIN RESPECT FOR SAUSAGES OR LAWS - SHOULD NOT WATCH THEM MADE"
OTTO VON BISMARCK

GROUPER BAKED WITH MELANGE OF FRUIT

1 grouper fillet (about 2 pounds)
1 large mango, peeled and cut into ½ inch pieces
2 bananas, peeled and cut into ½ inch pieces
3 peaches, peeled and cut into ½ inch pieces
1 pear, peeled and cut into ½ inch pieces
1 14-ounce can fruit cocktail, undrained
¼ cup Cointreau
lemon wedges and parsley sprigs for garnish

1. Preheat oven to 350°F.
2. Butter a baking dish large enough to hold grouper flat and place fillet in center. Top and surround fish with fresh fruit, canned fruit cocktail and Cointreau.
3. Bake 20 to 25 minutes or until fish flakes easily.
4. Garnish with lemon wedges and parsley.

Serves 6.

GRILLED YELLOWTAIL IN MANGO MARINADE

6 small yellowtail fillets (5 ounces each)
1 ripe mango, peeled, and pit removed
1 large and 1 small sweet Vidalia onion
1 clove garlic, minced
¼ cup olive oil

1. Rinse fish well with cold water and pat dry.
2. Purée mango, small onion and garlic in food processor. Add oil a little at a time while processing, or whisk in.
3. Pour marinade over fish and refrigerate up to several hours until ready to use.
4. After preparing the grill, put fillets, one layer deep, into covered fish grilling basket; add large onion, quartered, and fasten closed.
5. Grill 3 to 5 minutes each side, checking to be sure fish doesn't overcook. (Alternatively, the fish may be broiled).

Serves 6.

GROUPER BAKED WITH SOUR CREAM AND PINE NUTS

4 fillets fresh grouper (8 ounces each or 1 large 2-pound fillet)
½ cup butter, softened
½ cup sour cream
6 tablespoons shallots, finely chopped
1 tablespoon thyme or tarragon
4 tablespoons pine nuts or ⅓ cup almonds, slivered
1 cup dry bread crumbs
½ teaspoon salt
¼ teaspoon pepper
1 tablespoon parsley
¼ cup Parmesan cheese, grated
paprika
parsley sprigs as garnish
lemon wedges as garnish

1. Preheat oven to 375°F.

2. Rinse fish well with cold water and pat dry.

3. Blend together butter, sour cream, shallots, herbs, nuts, bread crumbs, salt and pepper.

4. Place fillets in baking dish, one layer deep. Cover with blended mixture. Top with Parmesan cheese and sprinkle with paprika. Bake 25 minutes and check for doneness. Fish should flake easily with a fork. Serve with parsley and lemon wedges as garnish.

Serves 4.

WHOLE FRIED FISH
WITH GINGER SAUCE

Fish:
1 whole fresh fish, such as snapper, approximately 3 pounds, scaled
    and gutted
Salt
½ cup all-purpose flour seasoned with ½ teaspoon salt and
    ¼ teaspoon pepper
3 cups vegetable oil

Ginger Sauce:
⅓ cup vegetable oil
4 cloves garlic, finely chopped
¾ cup pork, finely chopped
4 tablespoons fresh ginger root, finely minced
7 to 10 stalks celery or bok choy, cut on the bias about 3 inches long
6 scallions, cut about 3 inches long
*1 teaspoon ginger wine
*2 teaspoons Hoisin sauce
*2 teaspoons oyster sauce
1½ teaspoons rice wine vinegar
2 teaspoons sugar
¾ cup chicken broth or water
1 tablespoon cornstarch blended with ¼ cup cold water
scallion, diced (for garnish)

1. Trim any ragged edges on fins and tail of fish with scissors. Rinse under cold running water and pat dry. Wipe out and salt the cavity.

2. Lightly dust fish with seasoned flour. Heat 3 cups oil in wok or large frying pan. Carefully slide fish into oil and fry until crisp and golden on one side, about 3 minutes. Using 2 spatulas, turn fish carefully and fry on other side until golden. Immediately remove and drain excess oil; keep warm.

3. Heat ⅓ cup oil in wok and stir-fry chopped garlic 1 to 2 minutes, just until garlic turns yellowish. Add pork and stir-fry over high heat until meat is cooked to medium, about 2 minutes. Add ginger, celery and scallion; continue to stir-fry 4 to 5 minutes.

4. Reduce heat. Add ginger wine, Hoisin sauce, oyster sauce, vinegar and sugar. Stir.

5. Add chicken broth or water and bring to a boil.

6. Stir in cornstarch mixture and cook briefly. Serve immediately over whole fried fish. Garnish with diced scallion.

Serves 1 to 2, depending upon size of fish.

*Found in specialty food markets.

BROILED DOLPHIN WITH TOMATOES, ONIONS AND CAPERS

Served with Wild Rice Casserole, this is a crowd pleaser. Both can be prepared in advance.

4 fresh dolphin fillets (6 ounces each)
1 cup ripe tomatoes, diced
1 cup onions, chopped
4 tablespoons capers, slightly chopped if large
¼ cup fresh oregano, minced
¼ cup olive oil
1 clove garlic, crushed (optional)
4 tablespoons white wine (optional)

1. Place oven rack to highest position and preheat broiler.

2. Place fillets in shallow baking pan one layer deep. Top fish with tomatoes, then onions, capers, oregano and oil. If using garlic, spread over fish at this point.

3. Add wine (if desired) down sides of pan and broil 10 minutes. Check to see if any part of the inside of the fish is still uncooked. If so, put back under the broiler and continue to cook and check each 2 minutes. Do not overcook.

Serves 4.

BLACKENED FISH FILLETS

Fresh dolphin, cobia, tuna, snook and kingfish have been tried with this recipe. Serve with Spicy Spinach Rice Casserole and large salad for a tasty dinner party.

4 fillets or steaks of fresh fish, 5 to 6 ounces each
½ teaspoon onion powder
½ teaspoon garlic salt
½ teaspoon cayenne pepper
½ teaspoon basil
¼ teaspoon white pepper
¼ teaspoon thyme
¼ teaspoon black pepper
⅛ teaspoon sage
½ cup butter, melted
2 onions, sliced

1. Rinse fish well with cold water and pat dry.
2. Combine dry seasonings and set aside.
3. Coat fish with melted butter. Transfer to covered fish-grilling basket, one layer deep.
4. Sprinkle seasonings on both sides of fish; add onions and fasten basket closed.
5. Cook on hot gas grill 3 to 5 minutes each side. Do not overcook. Serve immediately, as fish continues to cook once it's removed from heat.

Serves 4.

Poultry

BEV'S ROASTED HOLIDAY TURKEY

The recipes on the next few pages provide the makings for a great holiday meal. The seasoned sausage and cranberry relish can be prepared in advance. A large, covered roasting pan, if available, provides moist, tender meat while considerably reducing turkey cooking time. If covered pan is not available, see alternate cooking directions.

1 16 to 20 pound fresh turkey
6 tablespoons butter, melted
1 tablespoon olive oil
½ teaspoon salt
1 teaspoon paprika
1 recipe Herbed Garlic Butter for Poultry (to follow)
1 recipe Seasoned Sausage (to follow)
1 recipe Homemade Sausage Stuffing, or Kay's Potato and Bread Stuffing (to follow)
1 recipe Giblet Gravy or Teper's Easy Gravy (to follow)
1 recipe Judy's Cranberry Relish (to follow)

1. Prepare Herbed Garlic Butter and your choice of turkey stuffing. Set aside.

2. Rinse turkey well, reserve neck, liver and giblets. Pat dry with paper towels.

3. Preheat oven to 325°F.

4. To stuff the turkey: Place in bottom of large, covered roasting pan, breast side down. Loosely fill neck cavity with stuffing and fasten skin shut with skewers or poultry lacing. Turn breast side up and carefully separate skin from breast meat with one hand. Try not to tear skin. Work Herb Butter under skin. Loosely spoon stuffing into breast cavity and cover the opening with an end piece of bread. (Place leftover stuffing in buttered baking dish and bake 35 minutes at 325°F). Fasten tips of drumsticks in the metal clamp provided or tie them together with string.

5. Combine melted butter, oil, salt and paprika; rub over surface of skin.

6. Cover and bake approximately 3 hours. Remove cover during last 30 – 45 minutes of cooking to brown. Turkey is done when legs move easily and juices run clear when thigh is pierced or, when meat thermometer registers 180°F. Insert thermometer into thickest part of breast without touching bone.

7. Begin stock for giblet gravy just after putting turkey in the oven.

8. When turkey is done, transfer from roasting pan to carving board and let cool approximately 20 minutes before carving.

9. In the meantime, make gravy from pan drippings and turkey stock. (See page 131).

10. Remove stuffing, completely, from turkey. Keep warm. Carve turkey and arrange on large serving platter. Garnish with fresh rosemary leaves and colorful vegetables. Serve with Marvelous Mashed Potatoes, Pearlized Onions, Sherried Yams with Walnuts, Judy's Cranberry Relish and corn cut from the cob then steamed.

TO COOK TURKEY WITHOUT A COVERED PAN:

1. Preheat oven to 400°F.

2. Line roasting pan with bread slices. Clean turkey and brush liberally with vegetable oil. Place unstuffed turkey breast side down in bread-lined pan and bake 45 minutes (to warm the bones and cavity of the turkey). This will help maintain moisture and evenly cook the turkey meat.

3. Remove turkey from oven; turn down temperature to 325°F. Stuff turkey as directed in #4 above, filling neck cavity first before turning turkey breast side up.

4. Continue to prepare and cook turkey as directed above for approximately 3 hours, uncovered.

HERBED GARLIC BUTTER FOR POULTRY

---

4 tablespoons butter, room temperature
2 tablespoons fresh rosemary, chopped
2 tablespoons fresh thyme, chopped
1 tablespoon poultry seasoning
2 to 3 cloves garlic, minced

1. Pound all ingredients together in mortar and pestle, or mix in blender.

SEASONED SAUSAGE

1 pound salt pork, rind removed
1 cup water
1½ pounds freshly ground, skinless, boneless chicken or turkey
1½ pounds freshly ground, boneless, lean pork
3 teaspoons ground rosemary
3 teaspoons celery salt
2 teaspoons ground sage
1 teaspoon marjoram
½ teaspoon salt
1 teaspoon black pepper, freshly ground
1 teaspoon dried thyme
1 teaspoon dried savory
½ teaspoon fresh nutmeg, grated

   1. Cut salt pork into ½ inch cubes, place in medium saucepan with water and bring to a boil. Reduce heat and simmer 12 to 15 minutes. Drain and purée in food processor or blender.
   2. Combine purée with other meats and seasonings. The sausage is best if chilled at least 8 hours or overnight for flavors to blend. At this point sauté 1 or 2 tablespoons of sausage in a small amount of oil to taste and adjust seasonings, if desired. Allow to come to room temperature before cooking.
   3. To cook, sauté in large skillet over medium heat 10 to 15 minutes. Drain and set aside.

Makes approximately 6 cups.

Note: *If used for Homemade Sausage Stuffing, you will have an extra three cups. You may use these in recipes that require seasoned chopped meat, such as in lasagna (see page 104). In which case, you would be replacing the meatballs and omitting the salt in the sauce.*

HOMEMADE SAUSAGE STUFFING

10 cups fresh bread, finely crumbled
3 cups light cream or milk
3 cups Seasoned Sausage (or market prepared sausage)
3 cups onions, slivered
1½ cups celery, finely chopped
1 cup pine nuts (or walnuts)
1 large carrot, pared and grated
½ cup fresh parsley, finely chopped
1 tablespoon each, of: ground sage, rosemary and savory
1 teaspooon each, of: marjoram, thyme, freshly ground pepper
pinch of cayenne

1. Soak bread crumbs in cream or milk and set aside.

2. Sauté sausage as directed in large skillet over medium-high heat 10 to 15 minutes. Remove sausage with slotted spoon and place in a large bowl.

3. In pan drippings, sauté onions, celery and nuts until onions are translucent.

4. Squeeze liquid from bread crumbs and add to sautéed, crumbled sausage. Add onion mixture, grated carrot and remaining seasonings.

5. Mix well and let flavors blend at room temperature at least one-half hour before stuffing turkey.

6. To cook stuffing separately, place in greased, covered casserole dish and bake in preheated 325°F. oven 45 minutes.

KAY'S BREAD STUFFING

6 cups whole wheat bread, toasted, and cut into 1 inch cubes
8 white potatoes, peeled and boiled until tender
½ cup butter
3 onions, chopped
4 stalks celery with leaves, chopped
1 egg
2 tablespoons parsley flakes
1 tablespoon celery salt
1 teaspoon sage
1 teaspoon thyme
freshly ground pepper to taste

1. Mix all ingredients together in large mixing bowl and stuff turkey as directed.

2. To cook separately, place in greased, covered casserole dish and bake in preheated 325°F. oven 35 minutes.

JUDY'S ORANGE/CRANBERRY RELISH

This can be made one week in advance and freezes well.

½ unpeeled orange, very finely chopped
1 cup water
1¼ cups granulated sugar
2 cups fresh cranberries, rinsed well
½ cup raisins
¼ cup walnuts, chopped
⅛ teaspoon cinnamon

1. In a large pot, combine orange and water and bring to a boil. Reduce heat to medium and cook about 20 minutes, or until peel is tender.

2. Add sugar, cranberries and raisins. Over medium heat bring to a boil, stirring occasionally, until sugar dissolves.

3. Increase heat to medium high and cook until berries pop and mixture thickens, approximately 15 minutes. Add nuts and stir to prevent sticking. Remove from heat and add cinnamon. Serve warm or refrigerate in an airtight containter and serve as desired with poultry or lamb.

Makes 2 cups.

GIBLET GRAVY

turkey giblets and neck, rinsed
2 tablespoons butter
2 onions, peeled and slivered
2 stalks celery, sliced
2 carrots, pared and sliced
1 bay leaf
4 sprigs parsley
Juice of half a lemon
1/2 teaspoon salt
1 tablespoon each of dried thyme, sage and savory
4 to 6 cups chicken broth or water, boiling
flour as needed

1. In large saucepan, sear neck and giblets in very hot butter. Add onions, celery and carrots; sauté 5 to 10 minutes.

2. Add remaining ingredients and bring to a boil, skimming the top if needed.

3. Reduce heat and simmer, uncovered, one hour and covered another two hours, or until giblets are tender.

4. Strain through a fine sieve into a bowl, pressing vegetables down with back of spoon to release all liquid and set aside.

5. After removing turkey from roasting pan, strain pan juices. Skim fat and return liquid to roasting pan.

6. Place roasting pan over medium heat, scrape bottom and sides to remove all browned pieces. Stir in strained, boiling liquid from giblets. Whisk in flour as needed to thicken gravy and cook over low heat 7 to 10 minutes.

7. Taste for seasoning and heat thoroughly while turkey is carved. Serve piping hot in a gravy boat.

TEPER'S EASY GRAVY ALTERNATIVE

To make gravy without using giblets, simply surround turkey in roasting pan, before baking, with 2 onions, chopped, 3 stalks celery, chopped and 4 carrots, chopped. When turkey is done, skim off fat from pan juices and purée ingredients in blender or food processor. Adjust for seasonings, heat thoroughly and serve in a gravy boat.

Thanksgiving Sunset

over the Miami Intracoastal Waterway.

TANGERINE CHICKEN

2 pounds chicken breasts, skinned and boned, cut into serving pieces
1 teaspoon cornstarch
½ cup onion, diced
5 scallions, cut into 1-inch lengths
5 dried chili peppers, minced
2 teaspoons roasted Szechuan peppercorns, ground
1 tablespoon fresh ginger, minced
4 tablespoons tangerine or orange juice
1 teaspoon lime juice
2 tablespoons dark soy sauce
*1½ tablespoons Hoisin sauce
2 teaspoons granulated sugar
*1 teaspoon Szechuan chili paste with garlic
2 cups olive oil
3 tablespoons fresh tangerine or orange peel, cut into strips
2 teaspoons white vinegar
2 teaspoons sesame oil

   1. Combine chicken and cornstarch. Set aside.
   2. Combine onions and scallions in small bowl. Combine chili peppers, peppercorns and ginger in another bowl. Combine tangerine or orange juice, lime juice, soy sauce, Hoisin, sugar and chili paste. Mix well. Set aside.
   3. Heat oil in wok to 225°F. Add chicken and cook until it loses its pink color. Remove chicken and drain. Pour out all but 1 tablespoon of oil.
   4. Heat oil until very hot. Add chili peppers mixture and stir-fry 15 seconds. Add peel. Add combined onion and stir-fry 20 seconds. Mix in chicken. Add juice mixture and stir-fry 30 seconds. Add vinegar and stir-fry 15 seconds. Mix in sesame oil and serve.

Serves 2 to 3.

*Found in Oriental groceries or in specialty section of supermarket.

SAVANNAH-BANANA CHICKEN

1 cup onions, finely chopped
1 clove garlic, minced
2 tablespoons unsalted butter
1 8-ounce can pineapple chunks, drained
3 heaping teaspoons apricot jam
¾ cup dark molasses
4 lemons, or ½ cup fresh lemon juice
2 tablespoons prepared hot mustard
1 tablespoon fresh ginger, grated
1 teaspoon salt
pinch Cayenne pepper
pinch cumin
1 broiler-fryer chicken (2½ to 3 pounds), cut up
4 bananas

1. Sauté onion and garlic in butter in large skillet over medium-high heat until soft, about 5 minutes. Stir in remaining ingredients except chicken and bananas. Heat to boiling then reduce heat and simmer, uncovered, 10 minutes, stirring occasionally. Cool to room temperature.

2. Arrange chicken pieces in single layer in shallow baking pan. Pour sauce over chicken and refrigerate, covered, one hour.

3. Preheat oven to 375°F.

4. Bake chicken, basting every 10 to 15 minutes with sauce, until almost tender, about 1 hour.

5. Peel bananas, cut into ½-inch thick diagonal slices and place between chicken pieces. Baste with sauce and bake another 10 minutes. Place chicken under broiler 2 to 3 minutes for a darker glaze.

6. Transfer chicken and bananas to warm serving platter. Degrease sauce, pour over chicken and serve.

Serves 6 to 8.

SOLDIER KEY CHICKEN BREASTS

¼ cup all-purpose flour
1 teaspoon salt
¼ teaspoon freshly ground pepper
5 large chicken breasts, cut in half and boned
6 tablespoons butter
3 tablespoons olive oil
1 clove garlic, minced
3 tablespoons Dijon mustard
1¼ cups milk
¾ cup dry white wine
¼ teaspoon dried basil leaves
red grapes and watercress for garnish

1. Preheat oven to 350°F.

2. Mix flour, salt and pepper in medium bowl. Dredge chicken breasts in flour mixture.

3. In large skillet heat 3 tablespoons butter and oil. Sauté chicken breasts, turning once, until golden, about 10 minutes. Arrange in single layer in shallow baking dish.

4. Melt remaining 3 tablespoons butter in medium saucepan. Add garlic and mustard. Cook until it bubbles. Whisk in milk, wine and basil. Cook, whisking constantly, until mixture thickens and bubbles for 1 minute. Pour sauce over chicken.

5. Bake covered until chicken is tender, 20 to 25 minutes. Arrange chicken on serving platter, spoon sauce over top, and garnish with grapes and watercress.

Serves 8.

CHICKEN PORT ST. LUCIE

3 ounces whole-milk Mozzarella, chopped
3 ounces Canadian bacon, chopped
1½ teaspoons dried basil, crumbled
4 small whole chicken breasts, skined, boned and flattened between
    sheets of dampened wax paper to ⅜ inch thickness
flour seasoned with salt and pepper for dredging
2 large eggs, beaten lightly
2 cups fresh fine bread crumbs
3½ tablespoons olive oil
3½ tablespoons unsalted butter
3 tablespoons scallion greens, thinly sliced
3 tablespoons fresh parsley, chopped
3 teaspoons fresh lemon juice, or to taste
salt and pepper to taste

1. In a small bowl toss together Mozzarella, bacon and basil. Spoon mixture onto half of each chicken breast and fold the other halves over it, pressing edges together.

2. Dredge chicken breasts in flour, shaking off any excess. Dip in eggs, coating well, and roll in bread crumbs, patting crumbs to make them adhere.

3. In heavy skillet heat oil over moderate heat until hot but not smoking. Cook chicken breasts in oil, turning once, for 10 to 12 minutes, or until juices run clear when chicken is pierced with skewer. Transfer to heated platter.

4. Wipe skillet with paper towels. Heat butter and sauté scallion greens over moderately low heat, stirring 2 minutes. Add parsley, lemon juice, salt and pepper to taste. Pour sauce over chicken and serve.

Serves 4.

OCEAN DRIVE CHICKEN THIGHS

3½ pounds chicken thighs, boned and cut into serving pieces
1 cup yogurt
½ teaspoon ground ginger
¼ teaspoon ground cloves
2 teaspoons dried coriander
1 teaspoon turmeric
½ teaspoon cumin
2-3 cloves garlic (according to taste), minced
salt and pepper to taste
fresh parsley sprigs as garnish
2 lemons, sliced, as garnish

1. Blend yogurt and seasonings in a bowl. Marinate chicken in mixture at least 3 to 4 hours in refrigerator.

2. Preheat broiler.

3. Place chicken on broiling pan and broil, turning at least once until well browned. Broiling time depends on size of pieces.

4. Place on serving platter and garnish with parsley and lemon slices.

Serve with Bulgarian Pilaf (see page 82).

Serves 6 to 8.

CHICKEN POT PIE

1 recipe Basic Pie Crust (see page 194)
3½ tablespoons butter
½ cup mushrooms, sliced
3 tablespoons flour
1¼ cups chicken broth
¼ cup white wine
1 cup boiled chicken, cut in bite-sized pieces
1 10-ounce package of frozen mixed vegetables, thawed
2 tablespoons combination of fresh herbs, chopped or 1 tablespoon
*   mixed dried herbs (such as: tarragon, chives, thyme, basil)*
1 egg yolk (optional)
1 tablespoon Sherry

1. Preheat oven to 350°F. Roll out and bake bottom pie crust shell according to directions in basic recipe.

2. Sauté mushrooms in ½ tablespoon butter and set aside.

3. In medium saucepan, melt remaining 3 tablespoons butter over medium heat and whisk in flour to make a roux. Slowly whisk in chicken broth and wine. When sauce is smooth and boiling add chicken pieces, mushrooms, mixed vegetables and herbs. Cook at reduced heat a few minutes, until sauce is thickened.

4. If using the egg, pour some sauce over beaten egg yolk, mix and return to saucepan. Stir, let thicken and add 1 tablespoon Sherry.

5. Pour in pre-baked pie crust; top with remainder of prepared pie crust recipe (optional) and bake 20 minutes, or until top crust is browned.

Serves 6.

HERBED GOAT CHEESE ROASTED CAPON

1 large whole capon, about 6 to 7 pounds
juice of half a lemon
1 tablespoon butter
4 shallots, minced
4 ounces Montrachet goat cheese
1 clove garlic, minced
4 tablespoons combination of fresh herbs, chopped (2 tablespoons
    thyme, 1 tablespoon rosemary, 1 tablespoon sage or tarragon)
    or 1½ tablespoons dry herbs
1 tablespoon olive oil
salt and freshly ground pepper to taste
½ teaspoon dried, ground thyme
paprika
3 onions, slivered (optional)

1. Preheat oven to 400°F.
2. Rinse capon well and pat dry with paper towels.
3. Coat cavity with lemon juice.
4. Melt butter over medium-low heat and sauté shallots 7 to 10 minutes.
5. Combine goat cheese, garlic, fresh herbs and shallots.
6. Carefully separate skin of capon from breast and legs with hands. Try not to tear skin.
7. Place goat cheese mixture under entire surface of separated skin.
8. Place capon on roasting rack in pan, coat outer surface with oil, salt, pepper, dried thyme and a sprinkling of paprika.
9. Spread onions, if using, around chicken.
10. Reduce heat to 325°F. and roast one hour, or until juice from thigh, when pierced, runs clear.
11. After cooling 10 minutes, carve capon and place on serving platter. Serve onions on same platter or pass separately.

Serves 4 to 6.

ROSEMARY CHICKEN CASSEROLE

1 fresh chicken, cut in 8 pieces
1 clove garlic, minced
2 tablespoons fresh rosemary, chopped or 1 tablespoon dry,
  ground rosemary
1 tablespoon butter, softened
salt (optional)
freshly ground pepper to taste
2 to 4 onions, slivered
¼ pound green beans
2 carrots, cut diagonally in 2-inch pieces
1 large or 2 medium potatoes, unpeeled, cut into 2 inch cubes
¼ cup dry white wine (optional)

1. Wash chicken and place in shallow, covered casserole dish.

2. Mix together garlic, rosemary, butter, salt if used, and pepper. Either top chicken with mixture, or place under skin.

3. Spread vegetables around, not on top of chicken, starting with potatoes, then onions, carrots and beans. This can be prepared to this point the night before serving, or just before baking.

4. Preheat oven to 325°F.

5. Dribble wine, if used, down side of casserole and bake 35 minutes.

Serves 4.

CORNISH HENS FLORENTINE

4 tablespoons unsalted butter
1 tablespoon olive oil
6 tablespoons shallots, chopped
¾ pound fresh mushrooms, chopped
¾ pound fresh spinach, rinsed and drained
2 teaspoons garlic, minced
½ cup ricotta cheese
2 tablespoons Parmesan cheese, grated
1 egg yolk
½ teaspoon dried thyme, crumbled
salt
freshly ground pepper
¼ cup pistachio nuts, coarsely chopped and toasted
2 rock cornish hens, split (or backbones removed)
6 small, new red potatoes

1. Heat 2 tablespoons butter and olive oil in medium skillet over medium heat. When foam subsides, add shallots and cook until softened, about 2 minutes. Add mushrooms and cook, stirring frequently, until liquid is evaporated and mushrooms are browned, about 7 to 8 minutes. Remove from heat.

2. Preheat oven to 400°F.

3. Place spinach in steamer over boiling water. Steam, covered, until tender, 3 to 5 minutes, and drain. When cool enough to handle, squeeze spinach as dry as possible and coarsely chop.

4. In medium bowl, thoroughly combine shallots, mushrooms, spinach, garlic, ricotta, Parmesan, egg yolk, thyme, ½ teaspoon salt and pepper. Stir in pistachios.

5. Place hens flat with skin sides up on work surface with drumsticks facing you. Carefully separate skin from breast meat with hands and work half the stuffing mixture under skin of each hen. Tie drumsticks together.

6. Heat remaining 2 tablespoons butter in small saucepan over low heat. Place hens, skin sides up and wings tucked under, in roasting pan with potatoes. Brush hens and potatoes with butter, sprinkle with salt and pepper to taste. Cook, basting every 10 minutes with pan drippings, until hens are golden brown and potatoes are tender, about 35 minutes. Let stand 5 minutes before serving.

Serves 2.

BARBECUE CORNISH GAME HEN

4 cornish game hens, split in half
Salt and freshly ground pepper to taste
⅓ cup orange marmalade
½ cup Madeira wine
¾ cup orange juice
2 tablespoons red wine vinegar
orange and lime slices as garnish

1. Wash hens, sprinkle with salt and pepper and place in a dish.

2. In a small saucepan melt marmalade over low heat. Remove from heat and add wine, orange juice and vinegar. Pour mixture over hens. Marinate one hour, turning frequently.

3. Either broil or charcoal grill. If grilling, make sure they are at least 8 inches from heat. If broiling, place on middle rung of oven.

4. Cook skin side down first for 15 minutes, then turn, brush with marinade and cook another 15 to 20 minutes until done.

5. Place on serving platter and garnish alternately with orange and lime slices.

Serves 8.

COUSIN MAUREEN'S CHICKEN LIVERS

1 pound fresh chicken livers
⅓ cup sugar
3 tablespoons onion, grated
⅓ cup Dubonnet or Sherry
¼ cup soy sauce
2 tablespoons olive oil
3 cloves garlic, minced
freshly ground pepper to taste
sesame seeds (optional)

1. Clean and separate livers.
2. Mix together sugar, onions, Sherry, soy sauce, olive oil, garlic and pepper; marinate livers in mixture at least 3 hours.
3. Place thin layer of sesame seeds in large skillet.
4. Pour in livers and marinade. Cook slowly over moderate heat until marinade evaporates.

Serves 4.

UNCLE BLACKIE'S BARBECUE CHICKEN

This chicken is sooo delicious you can't wait to wake up and eat it cold – the next day!

1 chicken, cut into 8 pieces
⅓ cup olive oil
⅓ cup fresh lemon juice
⅓ cup soy sauce
1½ teaspoons fresh ginger, peeled and minced (optional)
3 tablespoons Sherry
1 tablespoon brown sugar (optional)
fresh pepper to taste

1. Mix marinade ingredients together and marinate chicken 3 hours or all day in refrigerator.

2. Barbeque chicken 40 minutes to 1 hour, periodically brushing marinade on chicken. Turn frequently or use rotisserie.

Serves 4.

Meats

BAL HARBOUR TENDERLOIN

1 whole beef tenderloin, trimmed (approximately 7 pounds)
1 cup Dijon mustard
1 clove garlic, minced
¼ cup olive oil
½ cup dry red wine
½ cup combination of fresh herbs (such as thyme, oregano and basil), chopped
additional fresh herbs as garnish

1. Rinse tenderloin, pat dry with paper towels and place in roasting pan.

2. Combine remaining ingredients and coat the tenderloin with mixture. Let set at least 1 hour, but overnight works best.

3. Preheat oven to 500°F. Place tenderloin into hot oven and reduce heat to 325°F. Roast approximately 40 minutes.

4. Remove and let meat stand 15 minutes covered with foil.

5. Slice and arrange meat on serving platter. Pour pan juices over meat and garnish with additional fresh herbs. Serve immediately.

Serves 6 to 8.

BEACH PARTY TENDERLOIN

1 whole beef tenderloin, trimmed (approximately 7 pounds)
¾ cup Dijon or Coleman's English mustard
½ cup honey
bacon slices (wrapped around tenderloin – to cover entire roast)

1. Pre-heat oven to 500°F.

2. Rinse tenderloin, pat dry with paper towels and place in roasting pan.

3. Combine mustard with honey. Mix well.

4. Coat entire tenderloin with mustard honey.

5. Wrap individual slices of bacon around entire roast.

6. Place roast in hot oven and reduce heat to 325°F. Roast approximately 40 minutes.

7. Remove bacon slices and broil until brown.

8. Slice roast in serving sized slices. Place on platter and garnish with bacon slices.

9. In small saucepan heat remaining honey-mustard sauce from pan and pour over meat slices, if desired, or serve separately.
desired.

Serves 6 to 8.

MEATBALLS IN RED-WINE SAUCE

These are marvelous, melt-in-your-mouth meatballs that go wonderfully with a broad noodle or a grain such as couscous.

For the sauce:
1 onion, minced
2 tablespoons vegetable oil
1 tablespoon flour
1½ cups beef broth
1½ cups dry red wine
1 teaspoon ground cumin
1 bay leaf
salt and pepper, to taste

For the meatballs:
2 onions, minced
¼ cup olive oil
1 tomato, peeled, seeded and chopped
1 jalapeño pepper, seeded and minced (wear rubber gloves)
pinch sugar
1 pound ground veal
1 pound ground sirloin
2 large eggs, lightly beaten
½ cup raisins
½ cup Parmesan cheese, freshly grated
2 cups fresh bread crumbs
salt and pepper, to taste
seasoned flour for dredging

1. To make the sauce: In a large skillet cook onion in vegetable oil over moderately low heat, stirring constantly for 3 minutes. Add flour and cook, stirring 3 minutes. Add broth and wine in a stream, stirring constantly, and stir in cumin, bay leaf, and salt and pepper to taste. Bring liquid to a boil, stirring, and simmer sauce 10 minutes. Set aside.

2. To make the meatballs: In small saucepan cook onions in 2 tablespoons olive oil over moderate heat, stirring 3 minutes, or until onions are softened but not browned. Add tomato, jalapeño, and a pinch of sugar. Simmer mixture, stirring 10 minutes, or until thickened. Let mixture cool. In large bowl combine veal, chuck, eggs, raisins, Parmesan, bread crumbs, tomato mixture, and salt and pepper to taste. Form mixture into two inch balls. Dredge meatballs in seasoned flour, shaking off excess. In large skillet brown meatballs in batches in remaining 2 tablespoons olive oil over moderately high heat. When browned, transfer to sauce.

3. Bring sauce to a boil and simmer meatballs, covered, 30 minutes. Transfer meatballs with a slotted spoon to serving dish and keep warm. Over high heat, stirring, reduce sauce by about one third and pour over the meatballs.

Serves 6 to 8.

STOVETOP BRISKET OF BEEF

4 large onions, slivered
2 cups chicken or beef broth, as needed
4 carrots, sliced
4 pounds first cut, fresh beef brisket
salt and pepper to taste
1 bay leaf
1 teaspoon crumbled thyme
2 tablespoons ketchup

1. Fill Dutch oven or heavy pot ¼" high with water or broth. Add slivered onions and simmer until onions are glazed, about 45 minutes.

2. Add carrots, then brisket seasoned with salt and pepper to taste, bay leaf and thyme.

3. Simmer four hours, periodically adding water or broth as needed.

4. Remove from heat and let stand two hours before serving.

5. Just before serving, re-warm brisket in oven or on stovetop.

6. Remove meat, slice thinly cross-grain and place on serving platter.

7. Add ketchup to gravy in dutch oven or pot, pour some over brisket and serve. Additional gravy may be served on the side.

8. Serve with Claribel's Favorite Compote (page 202) or horseradish as desired.

Serves 6.

ESPAÑOLA WAY VEAL CALVADOS

12 veal cutlets (3 ounces each), pounded thin
3 tablespoons flour seasoned with salt and pepper
½ cup unsalted butter
1 cup shallots, finely chopped
20 medium mushrooms, sliced
¾ cup Calvados
2¼ cups heavy cream
¼ teaspoon nutmeg
1 apple, peeled, cored and sliced
parsley for garnish

1. Dust veal with seasoned flour, shaking off excess. Melt butter in large skillet over medium-high heat. Add veal in batches and sauté until browned, turning once, about 4 minutes. Transfer veal to a heated platter. Cover, set aside and keep warm.

2. Add shallots to same skillet and sauté over medium heat about 1 minute. Do not brown. Add mushrooms, cover and cook about 2 to 3 minutes, stirring once or twice.

3. Pour off fat from pan. In a small pot warm calvados over low heat. Add to shallots and mushrooms, reduce heat and cook 5 minutes. Blend in cream. Place over medium heat and simmer until slightly thickened, about 3 to 4 minutes. Add nutmeg and stir gently. Spoon sauce over veal.

4. Garnish with apple slices and parsley. Serve immediately.

Serves 6.

VEAL MARSALA

1 pound veal scallopine
¼ cup flour
¼ cup Parmesan cheese, grated
salt and pepper to taste
2 tablespoons olive oil
½ cup Marsala wine
½ cup chicken consommé
2 teaspoons fresh lemon juice
pinch marjoram
pinch thyme
pinch sage
1 pound mushrooms

1. Pound veal to ⅛-¼ inch thickness. Cut into pieces 3 inches long and 1 inch wide.

2. Dredge veal in flour mixed with Parmesan cheese.

3. Sprinkle both sides with salt and pepper.

4. In large skillet, heat 2 tablespoons olive oil and brown veal on both sides. Add Marsala and cook 1 minute on high heat.

5. Transfer veal to warm serving platter.

6. Add consommé, lemon juice, marjoram, thyme, sage and mushrooms. Bring to a boil. Lower heat and simmer until mushrooms are cooked.

7. Add veal to mushrooms and Marsala sauce and heat 1 minute. Serve with rice or pasta.

Serves 2 to 4.

KEY WEST STUFFED VEAL

8 thin slices avocado
16 veal scallops, pounded thin
8 thin slices Monteray Jack cheese
10 tablespoons Parmesan cheese, freshly grated
8 ounces baby shrimp, cooked
flour for dredging
3 eggs, beaten
2 cups bread crumbs
*4 tablespoons clarified butter
2 tablespoons olive oil
2 teaspoons garlic, minced
2 tablespoons fresh key lime juice
¼ cup white wine
lemon wedges for garnish

1. Arrange 1 avocado slice over veal scallop. Top with 1 slice Monteray Jack cheese. Sprinkle with 1 tablespoon Parmesan cheese. Top with 1 ounce baby shrimp. Cover with another veal scallop. Pinch edges of veal together tightly to form a packet. Transfer to plate. Repeat with remaining veal, avocado, cheese and shrimp. Refrigerate until firm, about 1½ hours.

2. Dust veal with flour, shaking off excess. Dip into beaten eggs and roll in bread crumbs to cover completely.

3. Heat butter and olive oil in large skillet over medium-high heat. Add veal in batches and sauté until lightly browned, about 4 minutes per side. Transfer veal to a serving platter.

4. Add garlic to remaining butter and oil. Add key lime juice and wine. Simmer 1 minute. Drizzle over veal packets.

5. Garnish with lemon wedges.

Serves 8.

*Clarified butter: Melt butter in a saucepan very slowly. Let stand for half hour. Skim off white skin. Pour the golden liquid into a container with a lid and pour off sediment. Keeps 2 to 3 weeks in refrigerator.

HERB CRUSTED LEG OF LAMB

This coating is perfect for lamb chops, roast crown of lamb or roast leg of lamb.

6 pound leg of lamb
2 tablespoons soy sauce
2 tablespoons olive oil
½ cup Dijon mustard
3 tablespoons combination of fresh herbs, chopped, or 1½ teaspoons
*   dry (such as: rosemary, parsley, thyme, tarragon, marjoram)*
½ teaspoon powdered ginger
1 clove garlic (optional)

1. Preheat oven to 350°F.

2. Score the leg of lamb (make slits about ¼ inch deep on an angle – 3 or 4 cuts)

3. Mix soy sauce, mustard and oil together. Add ginger and herbs.

4. Using pastry brush, brush leg of lamb and portion scored with herb coating.

5. Roast 1¼ hours for medium pink or 1½ hours for well done.

Serves 6 to 8.

MOUSSAKA

3 large eggplants, unpeeled
½ cup olive oil (or more as needed)
2 large onions, chopped
1½ pounds ground lamb
¼ cup fresh parsley, chopped
½ cup full-bodied red wine
2½ tablespoons tomato paste
2 bay leaves
1 tablespoon fresh oregano, chopped, or 1 teaspoon dried
salt and freshly ground pepper to taste
½ teaspoon ground cinnamon
15 mushrooms, sliced
5 tablespoons butter
1 cup bread crumbs
1¼ cups Parmesan cheese, grated
3 tablespoons flour
2 cups milk
2 eggs, lightly beaten
1 cup cottage or ricotta cheese
pinch nutmeg

1. Preheat oven to 375°F.

2. Slice eggplant into ¼ inch thick slices and fry on both sides in olive oil. When brown, drain on absorbant paper.

3. In same pan, sauté onion and ground lamb until brown, stirring often. Add parsley, wine, tomato paste, bay leaves, oregano, salt, pepper and cinnamon. Blend well and cook until almost all liquid is absorbed.

4. Sauté mushrooms in 2 tablespoons butter and add to mixture along with 3 tablespoons bread crumbs. Mix well.

5. Butter a large casserole dish and sprinkle bottom with half the remaining bread crumbs. Add one layer of eggplant, then half the meat mixture. Sprinkle liberally with ¼ cup Parmesan cheese. Again add one layer of eggplant, remaining meat mixture and ¼ cup Parmesan cheese. Add final layer of eggplant. Cover with remaining breadcrumbs.

6. In a saucepan melt remaining 3 tablespoons butter and add the flour, whisking with wire whisk until flour is absorbed. Remove from heat and gradually add milk, stirring constantly. Return to low heat and cook until sauce thickens. Remove from heat and stir in eggs, cottage or ricotta cheese, nutmeg and ½ cup Parmesan cheese.

7. Pour sauce over entire casserole and sprinkle with remaining ¼ cup Parmesan cheese.

8. Bake approximately 50 minutes or until top is browned.

Serves 8.

RACK OF LAMB IN STOUT CREAM SAUCE

1 rack of lamb (6 or 7 ribs), trimmed and bones frenched
3 tablespoons unsalted butter, softened
6 ounces dark stout (beer)
3 tablespoons red current jelly
⅓ cup heavy cream
pepper to taste
orange slices and mint leaves for garnish (optional)

1. Preheat oven to 400°F.

2. Coat lamb with butter and place on rack of a roasting pan just large enough to hold it. Bake in middle of oven 10 minutes. Pour stout over lamb, basting with stout every 5 minutes, for 20 minutes more, and transfer to a heated platter.

3. Remove the rack from the pan, add jelly and cook mixture over low heat, stirring, until liquid is reduced to about 2 tablespoons. Add the cream, bring to a boil, and cook, stirring, until it is the consistency of thick cream.

4. Add pepper to taste. Serve lamb with sauce laddled over it.

5. Garnish with orange slices and mint leaves.

Serves 2 to 3.

LAMB WITH THYME

2 onions
*3 tablespoons balsamic vinegar
⅓ cup olive oil
¾ cup fresh thyme leaves
4 pounds half leg of lamb, boned
3 tablespoons vegetable oil
¾ cup dry Sherry
1 teaspoon garlic, minced
3 tablespoons Dijon mustard
parsley sprigs for garnish

1. Preheat oven to 325°F.

2. In a blender or food processor purée onions, vinegar, olive oil, and ¼ cup thyme.

3. In a large bowl, rub lamb with thyme purée and let marinate, covered. Chill 6 hours. Scrape off marinade and reserve.

4. Roll and tie lamb with string. In an oven-proof skillet, heat vegetable oil over high heat until hot but not smoking. Pat lamb dry and brown in oil.

5. Roast lamb 1½ hours or until a meat thermometer registers 140°F. for medium meat.

6. Transfer lamb to a platter and let stand, covered loosely, 20 minutes.

7. Discard fat in skillet, add Sherry and deglaze skillet over high heat, scraping brown bits. Boil Sherry until reduced by half. Add reserved marinade and simmer mixture, stirring 2 minutes. Stir in garlic.

8. Whisk in mustard and remove skillet from heat. Cover and keep sauce warm.

9. Remove string from lamb and discard. Slice and arrange lamb on platter. Spoon on sauce and sprinkle with remaining thyme.

10. Garnish with parsley and serve.

Serves 6.

*Found in specialty section of supermarket.

KAY'S LAMB STEW

2 pounds lamb shoulder, cut into 2 inch pieces
½ cup all-purpose flour seasoned with ½ teaspoon salt and
    ¼ teaspoon pepper
2 pounds veal and beef bones
3 tablespoons bacon drippings or 4 tablespoons oil
2 onions, slivered
1 clove garlic, minced
1 cup red wine (optional)
1 teaspoon salt
¼ teaspoon pepper
1 bay leaf
5 cups water
½ teaspoon each, of: thyme, sage, oregano and rosemary
2 cups potatoes, peeled and diced
1 cup green beans, cut into 1 inch pieces
1 cup carrots, sliced
1 cup corn kernels, freshly cut from cob or frozen, thawed and drained
1 12-ounce can tomatoes, undrained, puréed
2 tablespoons tomato paste
dash Worcestershire sauce

1. Coat meat pieces with flour seasoned with salt and pepper.

2. In large pot, brown meat and bones well in bacon drippings or oil over medium-high heat.

3. Add onions and garlic, stirring and scrapping bottom approximately 20 minutes.

4. Add wine, salt, pepper and bay leaf, stirring and retaining a simmer. Stir in water in 1 cup portions, allowing liquid to return to a boil after each addition. Remove any froth as it rises to the surface. Simmer one to two hours, or until meat is tender.

5. Turn off heat, remove bones and meat and let cool. Discard bones; break up and return meat to pot.

6. Add thyme, sage, oregano and rosemary. Bring to a boil then simmer, covered, one to two hours. Add potatoes, beans, carrots, corn, and tomatoes. Return to a boil; reduce heat and simmer 20 minutes or until vegetables are tender.

7. Add tomato paste and Worcestershire sauce; simmer 10 minutes. Serve with Cheddar Drop Biscuits (see page 178).

Serves 4.

SOUTH BEACH BABY BACK RIBS

1 rack of meaty pork ribs
1 teaspoon salt
pepper to taste
pinch allspice

Sauce:
1 cup tomato sauce
¾ cup onion, chopped
⅓ cup honey
¼ cup soy sauce
¼ cup olive or peanut oil
½ cup rice wine vinegar
1 clove garlic, minced
2 tablespoons brown sugar
1 teaspoon dry mustard
1 teaspoon Worcestershire sauce
1 teaspoon paprika
1 teaspoon sage
½ teaspoon pepper
⅛ teaspoon cayenne

1. Preheat oven to 300°F.

2. Sprinkle ribs with salt, pepper and allspice. Lie ribs flat in roasting pan, add 1 inch water and bake 45 minutes.

3. In the meantime, mix all sauce ingredients in a saucepan over medium heat and bring to a boil. Reduce heat and simmer 20 minutes. Set aside and prepare the barbeque.

4. Coat rack of ribs with sauce, and cook 10 minutes each side on the grill, basting with additional sauce as needed.

If desired, ribs may be broiled with sauce brushed over them and basted periodically.

Serves 2.

CALLE OCHO LOIN OF PORK

3 to 4 pounds pork loin roast, boned
¼ cup olive oil
2 cloves garlic, minced
¼ teaspoon ground cloves
1 teaspoon thyme
1 teaspoon sage
1 teaspoon basil
½ teaspoon paprika
⅛ teaspoon cayenne
3 tablespoons butter, softened
1 red onion, chopped
1 cup red wine
1 cup chicken broth or water
1 tablespoon flour (optional)

1. Preheat oven to 400°F.

2. Generously brush roasting pan with olive oil. Place roast in pan and roast 15 minutes.

3. In mortar and pestle or blender combine garlic, cloves, thyme, sage, basil, paprika, cayenne and butter. Blend into a paste and set aside.

4. Remove roast from oven. Make slits in roast 1 inch apart. Spread garlic mixture and chopped onion over roast. Pour wine into bottom of pan and put back into oven for 15 minutes.

5. Lower heat to 325°F. and continue to roast approximately one hour, adding water to pan as needed.

6. When roast is done, transfer to cutting board, cut into thin slices and keep warm on serving platter.

7. Place baking pan over stovetop burner, slowly stir in broth or water while loosening pan drippings. Whisk in 1 tablespoon flour to thicken gravy, if desired. Keep warm before transferring to gravy boat and serve immediately.

Serves 6 to 8.

Breads

BEV'S OATMEAL BREAD

4 cups boiling water
1½ cups rolled oats
*1½ cups steel cut oats (if unavailable substitute rolled oats)
2 tablespoons granulated yeast
1 tablespoon salt
4 tablespoons oil
½ cup molasses
8 cups unbleached all-purpose flour
¾ cup sunflower seeds
¾ cup sesame seeds
cornmeal flour for dusting pans (optional)

1. In bowl of electric mixer, combine water and oats. Let cool 30 minutes.

2. Sprinkle yeast evenly on top of oats. Add salt, oil, molasses and 2 cups flour.

3. With dough hook, mix 7 to 10 minutes on low speed or kneading setting while slowly adding remaining flour. Mix in seeds. If kneading by hand, do so for 15 to 20 minutes, on a well floured surface.

4. Cover dough with clean, warm, moist cloth and let rise 1½ to 2 hours.

5. Grease 2 large loaf pans and lightly sprinkle with cornmeal flour.

6. Place dough in pans and let rise another 30 to 40 minutes. Preheat oven to 350°F.

7. Bake 45 minutes, or until toothpick inserted into center comes out clean.

*Found in specialty supermarkets or health food stores.

Makes 2 loaves.

AUNT DEL'S DATE NUT BREAD

For so many years Bev's mom and Aunt Del kept this recipe a secret despite constant requests for it. It was their standard gift giving fare and now it can be yours.

1 cup strong coffee, boiling
1 cup dates, chopped
1 teaspoon baking soda
1½ cups all-purpose flour
pinch salt
1 tablespoon butter
1 cup granulated sugar
1 egg
1 cup walnuts, chopped
1 teaspoon vanilla extract

1. Preheat oven to 275 – 300°F.
2. Pour coffee on dates. Add soda and set aside.
3. Sift flour and salt together and set aside.
4. Using either an electric mixer or simply a fork, cut butter into sugar in a bowl; add egg and mix well.
5. In thirds, alternately mix flour and date mixture into sugar, beginning and ending with flour mixture, until all ingredients are combined.
6. Stir in nuts and vanilla.
7. Grease and flour an 8 x 5 x 3-inch loaf pan; transfer batter to pan and spread evenly.
8. Bake 1½ hours, or a bit less, if firm to the touch and a toothpick comes out clean when inserted.

Makes 1 loaf.

HAWAIIAN LEMON BREAD

½ cup butter
1 cup sugar
2 eggs, beaten lightly
1 lemon rind, grated
2 cups all-purpose flour, sifted
2½ teaspoons baking powder
1 teaspoon salt
¾ cup milk
½ cup walnuts, chopped
1 cup shredded coconut, toasted
2 tablespoons fresh lemon juice
5 tablespoons confectioner's sugar

1. Preheat oven to 350°F. (325°F. if using a glass pan).

2. In large bowl of electric mixer cream together butter and ¾ cup sugar until light and fluffy. Add eggs and lemon rind; beat well.

3. Sift together flour, baking powder and salt. Add to creamed mixture alternately with milk, beginning and ending with dry ingredients.

4. Stir in walnuts and coconut by hand.

5. Pour into greased 8½ x 4½ x 3-inch loaf pan; spread batter towards sides of pan to prevent lumping in center as bread rises. Bake 55 minutes, or until a toothpick inserted into center comes out clean.

6. Combine lemon juice and confectioner's sugar. Spoon over hot bread immediately after removing from oven.

Makes 1 loaf.

TROPICAL FRUIT MUFFINS

2 cups canned fruit cocktail, undrained
1½ cups granulated sugar
2 eggs
2 cups all-purpose flour
2 teaspoons baking soda
¼ cup brown sugar
1 cup walnuts or pecans, chopped
½ teaspoon cinnamon
¼ teaspoon nutmeg

Icing:
½ cup butter
¾ cup granulated sugar
½ cup evaporated milk
1 cup flaked coconut

   1. Preheat oven to 325°F. Purée fruit cocktail and liquid.
   2. Mix together fruit cocktail purée, sugar, eggs, flour and baking soda. Pour into lightly greased muffin tins ⅔ full.
   3. Mix brown sugar, nuts and spices together. Sprinkle on top of batter.
   4. Bake 35 minutes.
   5. To make icing; combine butter, sugar and milk in saucepan and bring to a boil. Simmer 2 minutes; add coconut. Spoon icing over muffins as soon as muffins are removed from oven. Serve with breakfast, brunch or lunch.

Makes 18 muffins.

GRANOLA

2 cups rolled oats
*1 cup unsweetened, flaked coconut
½ cup sesame seeds
½ cup sunflower seeds
¾ cup raisins
1 teaspoon cinnamon
½ teaspoon nutmeg

1. Preheat oven to 300°F.
2. Toast oats in oven on cookie sheet 30 minutes or until brown, stirring frequently.
3. Place remaining ingredients in large bowl.
4. Add toasted oats and toss until well mixed.
5. When cooled, store in airtight container.

Makes 4 cups.

YOGURT TOPPING FOR GRANOLA:
3 cups plain, unflavored yogurt
1 cup apple, cranberry, grape or orange juice

1. Mix yogurt with choice of juice and use instead of milk on granola.

*Found in specialty supermarkets or health food stores.

MONKEY JUNGLE BANANA BREAD

2 large eggs
⅓ cup heavy cream
⅓ cup vegetable oil
2 cups all-purpose flour
1 teaspoon baking powder
1 teaspoon baking soda
½ teaspoon salt
3 ripe medium-sized bananas
¾ cup granulated sugar
¾ cup dark brown sugar
1 cup currants
¼ teaspoon nutmeg
¼ teaspoon cinnamon
½ cup confectioner's sugar

1. Preheat oven to 350°F. Grease a 9 x 5-inch loaf pan.

2. Beat eggs, cream and oil together with a beater until well combined. Set aside.

3. Combine flour, baking powder, baking soda and salt. Set aside.

4. Slice bananas and whip together with granulated and brown sugars until creamy. Slowly pour egg mixture into sugared bananas, bit by bit. Beat 1 or 2 minutes. Add flour mixture and continue beating 1 or 2 minutes longer.

5. Add currants, nutmeg and cinnamon. Blend well.

6. Pour batter into greased pan and bake 55 minutes, or until a toothpick inserted into bread comes out clean.

7. Sift confectioner's sugar on top of cooled bread.

Makes 1 loaf.

INDIAN RIVER ORANGE LOAF

1 medium orange
2¼ cups all-purpose flour
1½ teaspoons double-acting baking powder
¾ teaspoon salt
1½ cups plus 2 tablespoons sugar
¾ cup butter
3 eggs
¾ cup milk
1 teaspoon vanilla extract

Drizzle Icing:
1 cup confectioner's sugar
2 tablespoons milk
1 tablespoon butter, melted
1 teaspoon vanilla extract

1. Preheat oven to 350°F.

2. Grate 1 tablespoon orange peel and set aside. Squeeze 4½ teaspoons orange juice and also set aside.

3. Grease 9 x 5-inch loaf pan.

4. In large bowl mix flour, baking powder, salt and 1½ cups sugar with a fork.

5. With pastry blender or 2 knives used scissor fashion, cut in butter until mixture resembles coarse crumbs. Stir in peel.

6. In small bowl beat eggs slightly with fork and stir in milk. Combine with flour mixture just until flour is moistened. Stir in vanilla.

7. Bake 1¼ hours or until firm to the touch and a toothpick comes out clean when inserted. Cool in pan on wire rack 10 minutes.

8. Remove from pan.

9. In 1 quart saucepan over medium high heat, heat orange juice and 2 tablespoons sugar to boiling point. Cook, stirring, until slightly thickened, about 5 minutes.

10. With pastry brush, evenly brush sugar mixture on top of bread.

11. Mix all Drizzle Icing ingredients together. Stir well. Drizzle atop cooled loaf.

Makes 1 loaf.

CHEDDAR DROP BISCUITS

These are mandatory with Kay's Lamb Stew and delicious any time with honey.

2 cups unbleached all-purpose flour
2 teaspoons double-acting baking powder
1 teaspoon salt
½ cup plus 2 tablespoons softened butter (10 tablespoons)
⅔ cup milk
¾ cup sharp cheddar cheese, grated
flour for dusting
butter for dotting biscuit tops

1. Preheat oven to 400°F. Grease and flour an 8 x 8 x 2-inch baking dish.

2. Sift dry ingredients into a bowl. Cut in butter or shortening until it resembles coarse meal. Stir in milk then cheese and blend lightly.

3. Roll approximately 1 tablespoon of dough into a ball between floured hands and drop close together into the baking dish. (Biscuits will pull apart nicely after baking).

4. Spread a little softened butter on tops of biscuits and bake approximately 20 minutes, or until tops are browned.

Makes 24 biscuits.

SOUTH POINTE POPOVERS

1 cup milk, room temperature
1 cup all-purpose flour
2 eggs, room temperature
1 tablespoon butter, melted
¼ to ½ cup butter for greasing

1. Preheat oven to 425°F.

2. Beat together milk, flour, eggs and 1 tablespoon melted butter until consistency of whipping cream. Do not overbeat.

3. Butter popover cups and heat in oven about 3 minutes.

4. Put a little butter at the bottom of each popover cup and return to oven about 1 minute or until butter bubbles.

5. Fill each cup ¾ full with batter and place on middle rack of oven.

6. Bake 20 minutes. Reduce heat to 325°F. and continue baking another 20 minutes. Serve immediately with butter.

Serves 6.

Desserts

STRAWBERRY GLAZED CHEESECAKE

2½ cups graham cracker crumbs
1¾ cups sugar
¾ cup butter
5 8-ounce packages cream cheese (40 ounces), room temperature
¼ cup sifted flour
¼ teaspoon salt
6 eggs, separated
½ cup sour cream (or ½ cup heavy cream)
¼ teaspoon nutmeg
1½ teaspoons vanilla extract
⅛ teaspoon almond extract
rind of 1 lemon
3 tablespoons lemon juice
1 recipe Strawberry Glaze (to follow)

1. Preheat oven to 325°F.

2. Combine graham cracker crumbs with ½ cup sugar and butter. Mix well. Press into a nine-inch spring form pan – sides first and bottom last. Bake five minutes – cool. Keep oven preheated to 325°F.

3. Cream the cream cheese at top speed of mixer 5 minutes. Add 1 cup sugar and mix well. Add flour, salt, egg yolks, sour cream (or whipping cream if preferred), nutmeg, vanilla extract, almond extract, lemon rind and juice. Whip until thoroughly blended.

4. Beat egg whites until stiff, gradually adding remaining ¼ cup sugar. Fold into cheese mixture.

5. Turn mixture into prepared graham cracker crust and bake approximately one hour. Turn off heat and leave in oven 40 minutes. Remove and cool in pan. Glaze as directed.

Serves 10 to 12.

STRAWBERRY GLAZE
1 quart fresh strawberries
⅓ cup granulated sugar
¼ cup water
1 tablespoon cornstarch
1 teaspoon butter
1 teaspoon strawberry or apricot jam

1. Wash and hull strawberries. Crush enough to make ½ cup and reserve remaining strawberries whole.

2. Boil crushed berries, sugar, water and cornstarch 2 minutes, stirring. Add butter and jam. Strain and cool.

3. Arrange whole berries over top of cheesecake and pour glaze over berries. Chill.

AUNTY GEILA'S BANANA NUT CAKE

½ cup butter, room temperature
1 cup sugar
2 eggs
2 cups unsifted cake flour
1 flat teaspoon baking soda
1 heaping teaspoon baking powder
1 cup milk
¼ teaspoon vanilla extract
2 ripe bananas, mashed
1 cup walnuts, chopped
1 recipe Butter Frosting (to follow)

1. Preheat oven to 350°F.

2. In bowl of electric mixer cream butter with sugar. Add eggs and cream well.

3. In separate bowl combine flour, soda and baking powder. Alternately add milk and flour combination to sugar mixture, ending with milk.

4. Fold in vanilla, bananas and walnuts.

5. Grease a 13 x 9 x 1½-inch baking pan (not Pyrex) and bake 30 to 35 minutes.

Serves 10 to 12.

BUTTER FROSTING FOR BANANA NUT CAKE

5 tablespoons all-purpose flour
1 cup milk
1 cup butter, room temperature
1 cup sugar
1 teaspoon vanilla extract

1. In saucepan whisk flour and milk together. Bring to a boil and cook, stirring constantly until very thick. Cool.

2. Cream together butter, sugar and vanilla. Add to cooled flour mixture and beat 20 minutes.

3. Spread over cooled cake.

MOISTEST CHOCOLATE BROWNIES

4 ounces unsweetened chocolate
1 cup butter, softened
1 cup sugar
2 large eggs
½ teaspoon salt
1 teaspoon pure vanilla extract
½ cup all-purpose flour
½ cup semi-sweet chocolate chips
confectioner's sugar for garnish

1. Preheat oven to 325°F. Grease and flour two8-inch square baking pans.
2. In top of double boiler, melt chocolate over hot water; cool.
3. In large mixing bowl, cream together butter andsugar.
4. Add eggs and beat well.
5. Gradually blend in melted chocolate, salt, vanillaand flour. Stir in chocolate chips.
6. Pour into baking pans and bake 30 to 35 minutes.
7. When cool, sift powdered sugar on top.

Makes 24 to 32 brownies.

THE ORANGE BOWL FANTASY

6 large oranges
1 pint sherbet (flavor is optional)
1 12-ounce package frozen rasberries, puréed
1 pint vanilla ice cream
whipped cream, for garnish
ground cinnamon, for garnish
6 fresh berries, such as strawberries or rasberries, for garnish

1. Cut off and discard top ⅓ of each orange. Remove pulp from oranges and freeze shells at least 1 hour.
2. Fill frozen shells to the top, in layers, with ice cream, rasberry puree and sherbet. Freeze.
3. Just prior to serving, garnish with whipped cream, sprinkle with cinnamon and a fresh berry.

Serves 6.

YO-YO SOUR CREAM COFFEE CAKE

2 cups all-purpose flour
2 teaspoons double-acting baking powder
¼ teaspoon salt
½ teaspoon baking soda
1½ cups sugar
¾ cup butter, softened
2 eggs
1½ cups sour cream
2 teaspoons vanilla extract
1 cup chocolate chips
1 cup currants

STREUSEL TOPPING:
1 cup packed brown sugar (light or dark)
¾ teaspoon ground cinnamon
½ cup cold, unsalted butter
1 cup walnuts

1. Preheat oven to 350°F. Butter and flour a coated Bundt pan. 9 x 13 inch baking pan.

2. Sift together flour, baking powder, salt and baking soda. Set aside.

3. Cream together sugar and butter and beat until light and fluffy, approximately 3 minutes. Beat in eggs, one at a time, beating 30 seconds after each is incorporated; continue beating 10 seconds. Add vanilla.

4. Alternately add flour mixture and sour cream, ending with flour mixture.

5. Mix in chocolate chips and currants.

6. To prepare Streusel Topping: In separate bowl combine brown sugar and cinnamon. Add butter, working it in with fingertips until it resembles coarse meal. Add walnuts.

7. Line bottom of greased Bundt pan with Streusel Topping and add cake batter.

8. Bake 50 minutes, or until a toothpick inserted in center comes out clean.

9. Let cake cool completely on a wire rack before inverting onto serving platter.

KIDS KARROT KUPCAKES

These are great for Halloween, school functions and children's parties.
1½ cups vegetable oil
1½ to 2 cups granulated sugar
4 eggs
2 cups unbleached all-purpose flour
2 teaspoons baking soda
1 teaspoon salt
2 teaspoons cinnamon
1 teaspoon nutmeg
3 cups carrots, grated
1 cup walnuts, chopped
1 cup raisins
2 teaspoons vanilla extract
1 recipe Cream Cheese Icing (to follow)

1. Preheat oven to 325°F.

2. Cream together oil and sugar in mixer. Add eggs one at a time, mixing well after each addition.

3. In separate bowl sift together flour, soda, salt, cinnamon and nutmeg. Slowly beat into sugar mixture and blend well.

4. Mix in carrots, nuts, raisins and vanilla.

5. Either use cupcake liners or grease and flour two cupcake tins and fill ¾ full with batter.

6. Bake 45 to 50 minutes and remove from oven. After 30 minutes transfer to wire cooling racks.

7. Frost with cream cheese icing when cooled.

Makes 24 cupcakes.

CREAM CHEESE ICING

8 ounces cream cheese, room temperature
½ cup butter, room temperature
1 16-ounce package confectioner's sugar
1 tablespoon fresh lemon juice
2 teaspoons vanilla extract
Decorations:
orange food coloring for Halloween
frozen blueberries or chocolate morsels for eyes
raisins for noses
sprinkles for hair
thin licorice strips for happy mouths.

1. Cream together well the cheese and butter in mixer.

2. Slowly add confectioner's sugar, mixing well. Add lemon juice, vanilla and food coloring (if desired, a dash of red and a dash of yellow makes orange). Frost cupcakes when they are completely cool and decorate (if desired).

Makes enough to frost 24 cupcakes.

LIVVY'S CHOCOLATE ROLL

¾ cup granulated sugar
6 tablespoons cocoa
6 tablespoons cake flour
1 tablespoon baking powder
5 eggs, separated
butter for greasing pan
½ cup confectioner's sugar

Filling and Topping:
1¼ cups heavy cream
1 tablespoon granulated sugar
1 teaspoon vanilla extract
1½ cups combination of bananas and strawberries
½ cup strawberries, sliced, for garnish
chocolate shavings for garnish (optional)

1. Preheat oven to 350°F.
2. Combine sugar, cocoa, cake flour and baking powder. Set aside.
3. Beat egg whites until soft peaks form, adding sugar a little at a time.
4. In separate bowl beat yolks until thick and fold into whites.
5. Fold dry ingredients into egg mixture.
6. Grease a 10 x 15½ x 1-inch jellyroll pan and line with lightly greased wax paper.
7. Spread batter evenly over wax paper, handling gently.
8. Bake 15 to 20 minutes.
9. Spread a large sheet of clean wax paper on counter or cooling rack and sprinkle with confectioner's sugar. Invert cake onto wax paper. Let cool.
10. Roll and refrigerate.
11. Whip cream with sugar and vanilla. Slice bananas and strawberries.
12. When ready to use, unroll cake, spread half the whipped cream, then sliced fruit over cake. Roll up and spread remaining cream over top of rolled cake. Garnish with strawberries placed down center of roll and sprinkle with chocolate shavings (if desired).

Serves 8.

MIAMI BEACH SANDIES

*½ vanilla bean, chopped
1½ cups confectioner's sugar
⅛ teaspoon cinnamon
1¼ cups walnuts or pecans
1¼ cups butter, room temperature
1 cup granulated sugar
2¾ cups all-purpose flour

1. Combine vanilla bean with cinnamon and confectioner's sugar. Cover and let stand overnight.

2. Preheat oven to 350°F.

3. Chop walnuts in food processor until a paste has formed.

4. In bowl, using fingers, mix nut paste, butter, granulated sugar and flour into a smooth dough. Shape dough, about a teaspoon at a time, into balls and flatten to ¼ inch in height.

5. Bake on ungreased cookie sheet until lightly browned, about 15 minutes. Cool one minute.

6. While warm, roll cookies in prepared vanilla, cinnamon and sugar mixture. Cool completely and store in airtight containers.

Makes 5 dozen.

*Pound vanilla bean in mortar or place on cutting board and pound with flat side of knife or mallet.

JOY'S PECAN SHORTBREAD SQUARES

1¾ cups butter
¾ cup plus 6 tablespoons dark brown sugar
1 egg
1 teaspoon vanilla
3 cups all-purpose flour
2 cups pecans
7 tablespoons honey
¼ teaspoon cinnamon
3 tablespoons heavy whipping cream

1. Preheat oven to 350°F.

2. In food processor combine 1 cup butter, 6 tablespoons brown sugar, egg, vanilla and flour. Process until dough forms.

3. Press onto ungreased jelly-roll pan and prick with fork. Bake 20 minutes and remove from oven. Keep oven heated.

4. Spread pecans on shortbread.

5. Melt ¾ cup butter, cinnamon and honey in saucepan over medium heat. Add ¾ cup brown sugar and bring to a boil, whisking constantly 5 minutes. Remove from heat and immediately add heavy cream.

6. Pour sauce over pecans, return to oven and bake another 20 minutes. Cool to room temperature, cut into squares or diagonals and serve.

CINNAMON SUGAR CRINKLES

These light, crispy, chewy cookies can barely make it to the cookie jar. Make sure no one is home while baking these – otherwise they usually go from the oven, to the hand, to the mouth!

¾ cups all-purpose flour, sifted
2 teaspoons cream of tartar
1 teaspoon baking soda
¼ teaspoon salt
1 cup unsalted butter, softened
2 cups granulated sugar
2 large eggs
1 teaspoon corn syrup
2 teaspoons vanilla extract
1 tablespoon ground cinnamon mixed with 1 tablespoon granulated sugar

   1. Combine four, cream of tartar, baking soda and salt, and sift again. Set aside.

   2. Cream together butter and sugar until fluffy, approximately 4 minutes. Add eggs, 1 at a time, beating well after each addition. Add corn syrup and vanilla and beat 1 minute more.

   3. Add flour mixture in 4 parts and beat thoroughly after adding each part.

   4. Cover bowl of dough with plastic wrap and refrigerate approximately 90 minutes.

   5. Preheat oven to 400°F.

   6. Roll dough into balls about the size of a walnut, then roll each in cinnamon-sugar mixture. Place about 2 inches apart on ungreased cookie sheets.

   7. Bake 8 to 10 minutes, or until just lightly browned, but still soft.

Makes approximately 36 cookies.

MY CHOCOLATE CHIP COOKIES

Marcia's husband likes crisp cookies and the children like them chewy. These seem to satisfy everyone.

1 cup unsalted butter, room temperature
¾ cup granulated sugar
¾ cup light brown sugar, firmly packed
1 egg
2 cups flour, sifted
1 teaspoon salt
1¼ teaspoons vanilla extract
2 cups chocolate chips (semi-sweet, bitter-sweet or white chocolate)

1. Preheat oven to 375°F. After 15 minutes reduce heat to 350°F.

2. Cream butter with granulated and brown sugars. Add egg and mix well. Do not overbeat.

3. Gradually mix in sifted flour, salt and vanilla.

4. Fold in chocolate chips.

5. Generously grease cookie pans.

6. Drop cookie mixture in well rounded teaspoonfuls 2½ inches apart on cookie sheets.

7. Bake 10 to 12 minutes, until edges are a light to medium brown and centers a pale brown. Watch carefully.

8. Remove cookies with spatula and cool on wire racks. Store in airtight containers.

Makes 48 to 60 cookies.

RUGELACH

Filling:
1 cup walnuts, ground
1 cup currants
½ cup sugar
1 tablespoon cinnamon
½ cup chocolate chip miniatures (optional)

Pastry:
8 ounces cream cheese, room temperature
2 cups all-purpose flour
1 cup butter, room temperature
2 tablespoons granulated sugar
1 teaspoon vanilla extract
flour for dusting
1 12-ounce jar apricot or other preferred jam

1. To make filling: combine walnuts, currants, sugar and cinnamon in mixing bowl. Add chocolate chips (if desired) and set aside.

2. To make pastry: combine cream cheese, flour, butter, sugar and vanilla in large bowl and blend well.

3. Divide pastry into four pieces, dust each with flour and shake off excess. Roll each piece into a 10-inch circle between sheets of wax paper. Refrigerate 1 hour.

4. Preheat oven to 375°F. Butter a baking sheet.

5. Spread each circle of pastry with jam. Divide filling among circles, spreading evenly. Cut each into 12 pie-shaped wedges. Roll up each wedge from large edge to point. Arrange on prepared sheet, point side down.

6. Bake until golden, about 20 minutes. Transfer to wire rack and let cool. Store in an airtight container.

Makes 48 pastries.

BASIC PIE CRUST

2 cups unbleached all-purpose flour
1 teaspoon salt
¾ cup (6 ounces) vegetable shortening, well-chilled
½ cup ice-water
1 egg yolk mixed with 1 tablespoon water (optional)

1. Sift flour and salt together. Cut in well-chilled shortening with knife or pastry blender.
2. Add just enough water to bind dough by making a small well in center, pour in water and lightly mix with fork. Only add as much water as needed to allow dough to form a ball.
3. Working quickly and trying not to touch dough, use wax paper to divide dough in half, wrap in wax paper and refrigerate at least two but no more than 24 hours.
4. Roll out as needed on floured surface to ⅛ inch thickness. Working quickly, roll from center out in different directions to form a circle, turning frequently.
5. To pre-bake a bottom crust for a shell, preheat oven to 375°F., roll out one-half recipe, line pie pan, trim edge to 1 inch of pan and fold and crimp edges using thumb and forefinger. Prick dough with fork and line with pie weights. Bake 15 minutes or until golden brown.
6. To freeze remaining half of recipe, either roll out and line another pie pan or carefully wrap, seal and freeze in a flattened circle. This dough freezes well up to two months.

Makes a two-crust 8 or 9-inch pie.

KEY LIME PIE

1 recipe, Graham Cracker Pie Crust (to follow)
3 eggs, separated
1 can sweetened condensed milk
⅓ cup fresh Key lime juice (substitute lime or lemon juice)
1 cup heavy cream
granulated sugar to taste
1 teaspoon Cointreau
1 teaspoon nutmeg

1. Prepare Graham Cracker Pie Crust and set aside.
2. Preheat oven to 250°F.
3. Beat egg yolks until thick. Fold in condensed milk and Key lime juice. Mix thoroughly.
4. Beat egg whites until stiff and fold into lime mixture.
5. Spoon into pre-baked graham cracker crust and bake 10 minutes. Cool and refrigerate.
6. After pie is cold, whip cream with 1 teaspoon sugar and Cointreau. Spread cream over pie and sprinkle with nutmeg.

Serves 6.

GRAHAM CRACKER PIE CRUST
½ cup butter
1¼ cups graham cracker crumbs
2 tablespoons cocoa
2 tablespoons granulated sugar
⅓ cup pecans, crushed

1. Preheat oven to 250°F.
2. Melt butter and mix with crumbs, cocoa, sugar and pecans.
3. Press evenly into pie pan and bake 8 to 10 minutes. Set aside to cool.

Makes 1 bottom crust.

FRESH BLUEBERRY PIE

Oh, fresh abundant blueberries baked in a pie – Oh, what a happy person am I!

4 to 5 cups blueberries
¼ cup cornstarch
¼ cup cold water
¾ cup boiling water
½ cup plus 1 tablespoon sugar
¼ teaspoon salt
1 tablespoon fresh lemon juice
¼ cup flour
¼ teaspoon cinnamon
⅛ teaspoon nutmeg
pinch cloves (optional)
1 tablespoon butter
1 egg yolk plus 1 tablespoon water
1 Basic Pie Crust Recipe (see page 194)

1. Rinse, clean and drain blueberries.

2. In one quart saucepan dissolve cornstarch in cold water. Add boiling water and whisk until smooth. Add ½ cup sugar, salt and ¾ cup blueberries. Cook over medium heat, constantly stirring and crushing berries against side of pan with back of slotted spoon. Continue to cook until mixture boils and thickens. Cool, add lemon juice and set aside.

3. Combine flour, cinnamon, nutmeg, cloves and remaining 1 tablespoon sugar. Using a spatula, fold dry ingredients into remaining berries, then fold in cornstarch and berry sauce. Set aside.

4. Preheat oven to 400°F.

5. Roll out bottom half of pie crust and line bottom of pie pan. Turn blueberry mixture into pastry lined pie plate and dot with butter.

6. Roll out top half of crust and cover blueberry mixture. Trim excess pastry (beyond 1 inch) with scissors and seal edges by folding bottom crust up over top crust. Crimp edges with thumb and forefinger. Cut 4 slits as vents and brush top crust with egg yolk beaten with 1 tablespoon water. Cover outer edge of crust with aluminum foil to prevent burning.

7. Bake 15 minutes. Remove aluminum foil and continue baking another 40 minutes. Let cool at least one hour on wire rack. Serve with vanilla ice cream, although freshly whipped cream is a winner, too.

Serves 6.

MOM'S BANANA CREAM PIE

A deep-dish pie pan is needed for this pie.

1 pre-baked pie crust shell (see page 194)
3 cups milk
½ cup sugar
½ teaspoon salt
1 cup plus 2 tablespoons unbleached all-purpose flour
2 egg yolks, beaten
2 tablespoons butter
1 teaspoon vanilla extract
6 ripe bananas
1 cup heavy cream
2 tablespoons confectioner's sugar
½ teaspoon vanilla extract

1. Roll out and bake pie crust shell according to directions in basic recipe. Refrigerate to cool.

2. In saucepan scald 2 cups milk over medium heat.

3. In separate bowl mix together sugar, salt, flour and remaining 1 cup milk. Stir into hot milk with wooden spoon, stirring constantly over medium-low heat 10 minutes or until thickened.

4. Slowly stir in beaten egg yolks and cook one minute longer. Remove from heat, add butter and vanilla. Set aside to cool.

5. Thickly slice bananas and stir into cooled custard mixture. Spoon into cooled prebaked pie crust shell. Whip cream with sugar and vanilla; pile onto banana mixture. Keep refrigerated.

Serves 8.

LEMON CITY MERINGUE PIE

1 pre-baked pie crust shell (see page 194)
1 cup milk
½ teaspoon vanilla extract
2 tablespoons granulated sugar
3 egg yolks (separated, reserving whites for meringue)
3 tablespoons cornstarch
1 tablespoon Cointreau
juice of ½ to 1 whole lemon to taste
rind of ½ lemon, finely grated
1 Meringue recipe (to follow)

   1. In saucepan bring milk and vanilla to a boil. Cover and keep hot.

   2. In bowl of electric mixer beat sugar and egg yolks with a wire whisk until mixture is golden yellow and forms a ribbon. Whisk in cornstarch.

   3. Strain hot milk into egg and sugar mixture, beating constantly with wire whisk.

   4. Pour mixture back into saucepan and bring to a boil, whisking vigorously 1 minute. Add lemon juice and grated rind. Pour mixture into pre-baked pie crust shell and let cool.

Meringue:
3 egg whites
⅓ cup plus 2 teaspoons sugar
½ cup confectioner's sugar

   1. Make meringue immediately before you are ready to use it.

   2. Preheat oven to 425°F.

   3. Beat egg whites in bowl of electric mixer until they stand in peaks. Beat in 2 teaspoons sugar.

   4. Continue beating meringue until quite stiff. Blend remaining ⅓ cup sugar with confectioner's sugar and sift over whites. Fold mixture with rubber spatula.

   5. Spoon meringue onto pie filling, smoothing with spatula and lifting peaks.

   6. Place pie in oven and bake 5 minutes or until meringue is lightly browned.

   7. Sift some confectioner's sugar over top and briefly place pie under broiler to give a light glaze.

Serves 6 to 8.

PERFECT PUMPKIN PIE

1 partially baked pie crust shell (see page 194)
3 cups pumpkin pureé (4 pound fresh, whole pumpkin)
⅔ cup sugar
½ teaspoon cinnamon
¼ teaspoon ginger
¼ teaspoon nutmeg
⅛ teaspoon cloves
2 pinches salt
3 eggs, lightly beaten
½ cup heavy cream
½ teaspoon vanilla extract
1 tablespoon molasses (or maple syrup)
1 pint heavy cream
2 tablespoons maple syrup

1. To prepare fresh pumpkin, preheat oven to 325°F. Cut pumpkin in half and remove seeds. Place in shallow baking dish large enough to hold both halves and add ½ inch water. Bake 30 to 45 minutes or until tender (microwave 8 to 10 minutes). When cool, remove skin and pureé pumpkin meat in food processor until smooth but not liquid.

2. Increase oven heat to 375°F. Roll out pie crust bottom according to directions in basic recipe and partially bake 10 minutes.

3. Add sugar, cinnamon, ginger, nutmeg, cloves, salt and eggs to the pumpkin pureé. Mix well. Stir in heavy cream, vanilla and molasses.

4. Transfer to partially baked pie shell. Line outer rim of crust with aluminum foil for first ½ hour of baking to avoid burning. Place on cookie sheet and bake 50 minutes to one hour, or until firm. Serve lukewarm.

5. Heavy cream whipped with maple syrup is a must – for the pie, not the waistline!

Serves 6 to 8.

SOUTHERN PECAN PIE

1 unbaked pie crust shell (see page 194)
¼ cup butter
1 cup brown sugar (light or dark)
3 eggs
½ cup light corn syrup
1½ cups pecans
1 teaspoon vanilla extract
1 cup heavy cream
1 teaspoon granulated sugar

1. Preheat oven to 375°F.

2. Roll out pie crust bottom for shell according to directions in basic recipe. Do not pre-bake.

3. Cream together butter and sugar. Beat in eggs, one at a time.

4. Stir in corn syrup, pecans and vanilla.

5. Fill unbaked pie shell and bake 40 minutes. Let cool.

6. Whip cream with sugar. Serve pie with whipped cream and/or vanilla ice cream.

Serves 6.

CLARIBEL'S FAVORITE COMPOTE

Jackie's mother says if you want something terrific to serve as a sidedish with brisket, chicken or beef, make this. All the girls do! Make one day before serving.

1 can (17 ounces) fruit cocktail
1 can (20 ounces) pineapple pieces
1 can (16 ounces) sliced peaches
1 can (16 ounces) pears
1 can (11 ounces) mandarin oranges
1 can (20 ounces) apricot pie filling (substitute any fruit pie filling)
¾ cup apricot or peach brandy and Cointreau, mixed
5 bananas

    1. Drain very well and mix together fruit cocktail, pineapple pieces, peaches, pears and mandarin oranges.
    2. Add pie filling, brandy and Cointreau.
    3. Mix well and let stand 1 day in refrigerator. Stir occasionally.
    4. Slice bananas and add to above just before serving.
    5. This is also excellent and elegant as a topping for ice cream or pound cake.

Serves 8.

FABULOUS FANNIE'S FRUIT CRISP

1½ cups unsalted butter, chilled
9 large Granny Smith or other tart cooking apples (about 3 pounds),
*   peeled, cored, cut into ¾ inch chunks*
9 large Red Delicious apples (about 4 pounds), peeled, cored, cut into
*   ¾ inch chunks (or substitute other sweet fruit or berries)*
½ cup granulated sugar (or to taste)
½ teaspoon ground cinnamon
1½ teaspoons vanilla extract
2 cups all-purpose flour
2 cups dark brown sugar
whipped cream (optional)

1. Heat ½ cup butter in large heavy saucepan over high heat. Add fruit and sauté, stirring constantly 5 minutes. Reduce heat to medium, stir in granulated sugar. Cook fruit, stirring frequently until liquid has evaporated. Remove from heat. Stir in cinnamon and vanilla. Cool briefly. Taste for sweetness.*

2. While apples are cooking, mix flour and brown sugar in medium bowl. Cut remaining 1 cup butter into small pieces and cut into flour mixture with pastry blender until mixture is crumbly and butter is well distributed.

3. Preheat oven to 375°F. Butter a 15 x 9½ x 2-inch baking dish or other large, shallow baking dish. Spread fruit mixture evenly in dish. Top with even layer of flour mixture. Bake until topping is set and golden and fruit mixture is bubbling, 45 to 60 minutes. Let cool on wire rack until lukewarm. Serve with whipped cream.

Serves 12.

*** Tip:** Fruit crisp can be made up to this point 24 hours in advance. Refrigerate covered. Let fruit warm to room temperature 30 minutes before completing recipe.*

GRETA'S CHOCOLATE MOUSSE

7 ounces fine semi-sweet Swiss chocolate
1 teaspoon Kirsch
4 eggs, separated
6 ounces heavy whipping cream

1. Melt chocolate with Kirsch and cool.
2. Beat egg yolks until thick and add to chocolate.
3. Whip egg whites until stiff and set aside.
4. Whip the cream, add to chocolate mixture and fold in egg whites.
5. Transfer to individual serving bowls and refrigerate several hours.

Serves 6.

CANDY CRISP WALNUTS

Delicious as a snack or simple confection.

3 cups walnut halves
water
½ cup granulated sugar
1 teaspoon cinnamon (optional)
⅓ cup water
4 cups peanut oil

1. In saucepan cover walnuts with 4 inches water and bring to a boil. Boil 7 minutes, drain in colander and run cold water over walnuts until completely cold.
2. Drain walnuts well and pat dry with paper towels. Set aside.
3. In wok or heavy skillet combine sugar, cinnamon (if desired) and ⅓ cup water. Bring to a boil, stirring constantly 1 minute.
4. Add walnuts and cook over high heat, stirring constantly for 3 minutes, or until liquid has evaporated and walnuts are glazed. Let walnuts cool one layer deep on a jelly-roll pan.
5. Wash and dry wok or skillet, add oil and heat over moderately high heat to 380°F. or until a light haze appears. Fry walnuts in oil in 2 batches, stirring 4 minutes, or until they are browned. Transfer with slotted spoon to marble surface or jelly-roll pans one layer deep and let cool completely. Walnuts keep for up to 1 week in an airtight container in a cool, dry place.

Makes 3 cups.

SOBE SABLES

These cookies are incredibly easy to prepare and keep well for weeks. They are not overly sweet, have a marvelous, buttery flavor and are perfect to serve with coffee or tea.

2 cups all-purpose flour
⅔ cup plus 8 tablespoons granulated sugar
¾ cup plus 2 tablespoons butter, room temperature
1 egg
1½ teaspoons vanilla extract
1½ teaspoons ground cinnamon mixed with 1½ teaspoons granulated sugar (optional)
confectioner's sugar (optional)

1. Combine flour and ⅔ cup sugar together. Using hands, mix in ¾ cup of the butter. Add egg and vanilla; continue kneading JUST until ingredients are combined.

2. Shape dough into a large roll (log shaped) approxmately 2 inches in diameter.

3. Sprinkle remaining 8 tablespoons sugar over a wooden board and coat the rolled dough in sugar. At this point, if preferred you may combine equal amounts of cinnamon and sugar and coat rolled dough with this mixture.

4. Wrap securely in aluminum foil or plastic wrap. Refrigerate 12 hours. (Can be refrigerated for days at this point.)

5. Preheat oven to 350°F.

6. Unwrap dough and generously grease cookie sheets with remaining butter.

7. Slice dough into ¼ to ⅜ inch thick rounds and place them 2 inches apart on cookie sheets.

8. Bake 12 to 15 minutes or until golden brown. Transfer cookies to wire rack and let cool.

9. For added sweetness, sift powdered sugar on top of cooled cookies.

Makes approximately 28-30 cookies.